This book is a remarkable
merely microwave old topi<
has, however, written a rath
our lives and look for real fr
is a delight to read, touching several areas of contemporary life such as
sports and film. John humorously and honestly considers life under the
sun. But, and I must warn you, this is a book that will challenge your
heart and its insistence in following bad paths. What would Judas do
with this book? I cannot say, but I hope that you take up and read.

Emilio Garofalo Neto

Senior Pastor, Semear Presbyterian Church and
Professor of Systematic Theology, Presbyterian Seminary of Brasilia and
visiting Professor of Practical Theology, Andrew Jumper Graduate Center,
Brasilia, Brazil

I've been in the book business for a long time, and it's easy to feel like
everything has been done before (because it pretty much has). That said,
I've never seen a concept like this. Perritt has taken an old idea (the daily
devotional) and given it a new twist as he illustrates both the relatability
and hopelessness in the life of Scripture's most famous villain – Judas
Iscariot. Perritt's meditations are steeped in Scripture and full of gospel-
saturated hope.

Ted Kluck

Award-winning Author, co-host of The Happy Rant podcast

Why would anyone want to spend a month with Judas Iscariot? Because
we have much to learn from him, as John Perritt shows in this helpful
and creative devotional. We have more in common with history's
greatest traitor than we may care to admit. But by reflecting on the
failures of Judas we can better see how we can become more like Jesus.

Joe Carter

Editor at The Gospel Coalition and Author of NIV's Lifehacks Bible

In What Would Judas Do?, John Perritt invites you to walk a month in the
sandals of the most despised man in Christendom. On this enlightening
and sometimes haunting journey you will come to better understand a
man whose faults at times feel uncomfortably familiar, bringing fresh
perspective to the phrase, "There but for the grace of God go I".

Chad Gibbs

Author of God & Football and Love Thy Rival

If you have never considered picking up a 31-day devotional on the life of Judas, you are not alone! This book is unique to be sure. But it will be profoundly beneficial for all who read it. John skillfully uses the life of Judas to help each reader understand the nature of true faith in Christ. Some will find this book to be a needed warning, others will find it deeply comforting, but all who read it will be pointed to Christ's finished work.

Jason Wredberg
Senior Pastor, First Baptist Church, Watertown, Wisconsin

If you think you have nothing in common with Judas Iscariot, think again – John Perritt proves it from Scripture. Find out where Judas went wrong and how you can avoid ending up like he did in this unusual and insightful book. "There, but for the grace of God, go I" will take on a new and deeper meaning, and your gratitude for the Savior and his cross will grow!

Bob Bevington
Co-Author with Jerry Bridges, *The Bookends of the Christian Life*

This is a thought-provoking book. How could someone be so close to Jesus, spend so much time with Him, hear the Son of God preach, witness miracles, and yet still miss Jesus? It's the question that the disciple Judas forces upon our hearts. In this clear and short devotional, John Perritt asks us to take a sobering look at our own hearts and recognize that "Judas" is not just "out there" but within us. But even better, John through Judas asks us to look away from ourselves to see and trust the beauty, sufficiency, grace and strength of the One who loves and saves sinners and traitors. And that is always a worthy and hopeful endeavor.

Brian Sorgenfrei
Reformed University Fellowship Campus Minister,
Mississippi State University, Starkville, Mississippi

One of the most challenging things about being a Christian is not getting bored by the Bible, even by Jesus. It all just gets so familiar. What John Perritt has done is to give believers a new perspective on faith, on following Jesus, and even on ourselves. The contrarian in me loves this – a look at Jesus through the eyes of His betrayer. And a look at our own relationship with Jesus through exploring theirs.

Barnabas Piper
Author of *The Pastor's Kid, Help My Unbelief,* and *The Curious Christian*

John Perritt

WHAT WOULD JUDAS DO?

Understanding faith through the most famous of the faithless

CHRISTIAN
FOCUS

Scripture quotations are from *The Holy Bible, English Standard Version*, copyright © 2001 by Crossway Bibles, a publishing ministry of Good News Publishers. Used by permission. All rights reserved. ESV Text Edition: 2011.

John Perritt is the Youth Director at Pear Orchard Presbyterian Church in Ridgeland, Mississippi. He has published articles for The Gospel Coalition and Reformation 21 and occasionally blogs on film and theology at www.reelthinking.us. He and his wife, Ashleigh, have four children.

10 9 8 7 6 5 4 3 2 1
Copyright © 2017 John Perritt

Paperback ISBN: 978-1-78191-809-8
epub ISBN: 978-1-5271-0021-3
mobi ISBN: 978-1-5271-0022-0

Published in 2017
by
Christian Focus Publications,
Geanies House, Fearn, Tain,
Ross-shire, IV20 1TW, U.K.

Cover design by Paul Lewis

Printed and bound by
Bell & Bain, Glasgow

CONTENTS

ACKNOWLEDGEMENTS

Let me first thank Christian Focus for giving me the opportunity to bring this project to fruition. As I state in the conclusion, this book was simply a concept when I submitted it – merely five chapters – so thanks for taking a risk on this. It was a joy to bring this to completion and I pray the Lord uses it in the lives of many.

Thanks to my editor, Sandra Byatt, for making this book more readable. Your questions and thoughtfulness make this a more useful volume.

Westminster Presbyterian Church and Pear Orchard Presbyterian Church need to be recognized by this work. The former was the church of my youth and many labored to instill the faith in me. The latter is the current church I serve and continues to be such a gift and blessing to me personally as well as my family. POPC, you have been such a faithful church to the Perritt household these thirteen plus years!

Dr. John Kwasny and Dr. Emilio Garofalo have been constant friends and encouragers in my writing. Both of you read early drafts of this and encouraged me to press on.

The theological institutions I attended, The Reformed Theological Seminary and The Southern Baptist Theological Seminary, possess godly men who faithfully pass the faith on to future generations. I owe a major debt of gratitude to these two faithful seminaries.

My grandmother 'Nanny' has faithfully loved me since my childhood. It was a blessing to grow up 'around the corner' from you and I look back with fondness on the many days after school I got to spend with you. My mother and father have been such faithful parents that ensured me of their love by their constant support and encouragement. The same can be said of my sister, Emily. Thanks for your spiritual nourishment and love growing up. To my brother-in-law, Kevin, you never knew that a passing comment to continue my pursuit toward publishing this book kept me going. I had given up on this project until you encouraged me to keep going. Each of you played a part in the authorship of this book.

As always, my faithful wife, Ashleigh, should be considered a co-author. There were many Saturday mornings where you watched the kids so I could stay focused. Your faithful love, support and sacrifice assisted in bringing this book to fruition. I could not do any of this apart from you. Thank you for truly being my best friend.

To my children. You are some of the greatest treasures I could ever have. Sarah, Samuel, Jillian, Will, and Amber, you make me a better man and bring joy to my heart on a daily basis. I fail you as a father daily, but I pray God gives me the grace to grow into a more faithful father. Your daddy loves each of you so much and prays that you'll each fall in love with the only faithful Father.

Lastly, all of my writing is done for King Jesus. I am a broken sinner who has mixed motives in everything I do, but I pray my work is for our Triune God and the advancement of His Kingdom. As this book deals with faith and the doubt that can creep into each believer's heart, I pray that it only highlights the faithfulness of our ever-faithful Savior, Jesus Christ. To Him be all glory!

"[Judas] is the most colossal failure in all of human history. He committed the most horrible, heinous act of any individual, ever. He betrayed the perfect, sinless, holy Son of God for a handful of money. His dark story is a poignant example of the depths to which the human heart is capable of sinking."[1]

- John MacArthur

Aren't you glad you're not like Judas,
Selling the Messiah for a little bit of silver?
But wait.
You are like [him], and so am I.
There is simply no denying it.[2]

- Paul Tripp

---

1. John MacArthur, *Twelve Ordinary Men: How the Master Shaped His Disciples for Greatness, and What He Wants to Do with You.* (Thomas Nelson, Nashville, TN: 2002), p. 181.

2. Paul Tripp, *Whiter than Snow: Meditations on Sin and Mercy;* (Crossway Books, Wheaton, Ill. 2008), page 38.

INTRODUCTION

Judas Iscariot has always been an intriguing person to me. To be honest, I feel a bit sorry for him. He is a sad, pitiful character. He was influenced by the world. A worrier. Confused. Maybe I feel for him because he seems to be a lot like me.

Regardless of how you feel about Judas, he serves as a sobering reminder in God's Word. Not only do we deal with many of the same struggles Judas had, we can identify with his lifestyle. Judas, most likely, would have been sitting in the pew next to you at church. More than that, he would have been a leader in it. Growing up he would have stood out in the youth group. Playing guitar on the music team. Serving on mission trips.

Even though he would have appeared to be the cream of the crop of Christians on the outside, he missed out on an eternity with the One he appeared to serve. To put it bluntly, he has been suffering in hell for thousands of years and he will remain there for all eternity. I do not say that lightly. As Christians we can often be hesitant to speak of hell. However, it is a reality. A reality we don't like to consider but one that is a reminder to us while we are on earth. Scripture constantly calls us to think about the next life and Judas' life can assist us with that.

In J.C. Ryle's classic work *Holiness*, he says something about Lot that can easily be applied to Judas. 'The Holy Scriptures, which were written for our learning, contain beacons as well as patterns. They show us examples of what we should avoid, as well as examples of what we should follow.'[1]

Judas is a beacon to us. A beacon of what we should avoid, but his life is one of the most unique examples we have in all of Scripture. He not only had the appearance of a Christian, but was a leader for the Christian faith even though he never truly had faith. What can we learn from this beacon in Scripture that can assist us in our faith? God ordained the life of Judas for a reason, so let's reflect a bit on what that life can teach us.

This book is not designed to move anyone towards doubting their faith in Jesus Christ, rather it is designed to deepen it. Even though its aim is to deepen your assurance of faith, I hope this book makes you uncomfortable. The truth is, we are typically too comfortable in the Christian life. While we all know the Christian life is one of inconsistency, there should also be fruit we are striving for through the power of the Holy Spirit. It is my hope that this book will spur Christians on in the Christian fight. That it will produce fruit in your life that will move you towards a life like the

---

1. J.C. Ryle, *Holiness* (Charles Nolan Publishers, 2001 [First published 1877]), p. 178.

one Peter describes when he said, 'Therefore, brothers, be all the more diligent to make your calling and election sure, for if you practice these qualities you will never fall' (2 Pet.1:10).

Peter is exhorting Christians to a diligent faith. A faith that is not dependent on works, but a faith that is producing works. I hope that reflection upon the life of Judas produces in us a faith that takes the sacrifice of our Savior seriously.

There will be some liberties taken in this book. While I do not say anything that opposes Scripture, there is only so much we know about Judas. Therefore, there are assumptions made about his early life, his service as a disciple and some of what he thought. However, those assumptions are based on the Scriptural fact that we know he was a disciple of Jesus Christ and we know the lie that ultimately led to his destruction.

You can use this book in many different ways. It can easily be adapted for small groups or even a Sunday School class. Its primary focus is personal devotion. There are 31 reflections on the life of Judas which are designed to be read on a daily basis. Most benefit would come from focusing on one daily, along with prayer and in addition to reading Scripture. That being said, it is your book so adapt it to however it fits best with your devotional life.

Let me leave you with one final thought and it is a thought I believe Judas would want to leave us with:

Your life, however great and glorious it may be right now, will soon be over. You may be respected among others. You may be rich. You may be smart, athletic or good-looking. You may be very comfortable and content with the life allotted to you. But, there is another life to come. A life that never ends. A life that can be spent in perfect peace and rest in the arms of Jesus Christ, or a life separated from Him. The latter is the life I chose. It is a life filled with constant terror, constant suffering, constant anxiety, despair, worry and loss. It is a life that moves me to seek death each and every day, but the luxury of death is not offered here. While on earth I was with the Savior, but I did not recognize Him as so. I know now, He was my King. I know now, that He possessed true life. Turn to Him before you join me

DAY 1

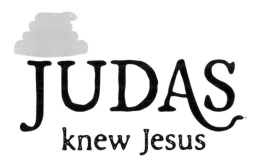

JUDAS
knew Jesus

'Even the demons believe - and shudder!' (James 2:19).

Judas knew Jesus better than you do. Does that scare you? He was called as one of the twelve (Matt. 10:4) and given authority by Christ Himself (Matt. 10:1). But the knowledge Judas had was not just a head knowledge (like many of us), it was a deep intimacy.

Judas traveled with Jesus from town-to-town. Have you ever traveled with anyone? Think about one of your favorite road trips, or perhaps your last family trip in the car (or minivan). There's usually a lot of excitement about a trip. Much of that excitement, however, goes away on the trip back home. You're tired. You're sad because the vacation is over. And, you've been around each other a really long time (some people might even smell funny).

What we know to be true is this. When you're around someone for a long time, you get to really know them. Not just the person they can often act like, but the person they really are. People speak more bluntly, the gracious actions towards one another may stop and people just begin to put self before service.

Well, Judas saw Jesus tired. Judas saw Jesus mobbed by people. Judas sat around Jesus by a fire at night. Judas knew Jesus intimately. He spent plenty of time with Jesus to understand who He really was. He saw Jesus wait on the lesser in the kingdom. He saw Him love the widowed and orphaned. He saw Jesus serve when it was inconvenient. He saw a fatigued Jesus who still showed love. Judas knew all of this about Jesus and he still chose thirty pieces of silver to betray him.

What Judas knew about Jesus would be similar to what you know about your closest earthly relationships. Think of the flaws you have been able to see in your siblings, friends, spouse or parents. The reason you see these flaws is not only due to the fact that they are sinners, but because you really know them. However, we see that Judas' deep knowledge of Jesus still did not save him.

What about you?
What do you know about Jesus? Are you simply able to rattle off some facts about Him? His earthly parents were Mary and Joseph. He walked on water. He is the second person of the trinity. Or, is your knowledge of Jesus something deeper? Is your knowledge of your Savior producing a nearness to your Savior? How can you really be sure your knowledge gets you any closer to Jesus than Judas'?

So many people these days want to *experience* Jesus. They want to feel His presence. Get a warm feeling about Him on the inside. Well, Judas experienced Jesus' true presence. Judas felt Jesus' warm hands washing his own feet, and this still wasn't enough for him to truly know Jesus. If Judas illustrates one thing for us, it is the fact that there is a difference between knowing Jesus and truly *knowing* Jesus.

In the Bible the word 'know' often refers to a deep intimacy. Often an intimacy reserved for husband and wife (Gen. 4:1). So while we can say that Judas intimately knew Jesus, he did not know Him in a way that leads to salvation. However, what does that mean for you or me? How do we know that we really know Jesus? Should we just believe harder? Place our faith in Him more?

In Galatians 4:9 Paul states, 'But now that you have come to know God, or rather to be known by God, how can you turn back again to the weak and worthless elementary principles of the world, whose slaves you want to be once more?'

In a sense, your knowledge of Jesus will always be more limited than Judas' knowledge. Judas knew Jesus by sight and we know Him by faith. It isn't until our last day that our faith becomes sight. However, as Tim Keller states, 'What makes a person a Christian is not so much your knowing of God but His knowing of you.'[1] Our faith changes, depending on the season of life. Sometimes you're happy, sometimes you're sad, sometimes you're indifferent. Truth be told, sometimes you don't know what you believe.

Paul reminds us that God knows us fully and still loves us. He knows your thoughts, your words and your deeds and it does not change His steadfast love. This is unlike any other

1. Tim Keller, *Galatians For You* (The Good Book Company, 2013), p. 106.

relationship you have. Remember, Jesus knew you were His enemy when He left the throne to come and save you.

Imagine if you shared ALL of your thoughts and desires with everyone. If you shared every thought that came into your mind, even with your closest friends and family, they would have a hard time loving you. With Jesus, however, His love for you doesn't change based on what He knows about you. Understanding this, already puts your knowledge of Christ ahead of Judas'.

Here's the bottom line, *a true understanding of Jesus' knowledge of you will shape your knowing of Him*. To say it another way, the more you understand your brokenness, the more you love the man, Jesus Christ. Or, to say it how John Calvin once did, *to know self, one must know God*. That is, once you more deeply know your sin and brokenness, you more deeply rest in the arms of the One who can deliver you from it.

And this is a distinction Judas never came to grasp. Yes, Judas knew Jesus, but Judas never truly knew *Judas*. Through their traveling he got to know Jesus intimately, but he didn't really know himself. Judas didn't know his sin. Judas didn't know his selfishness. And, because he didn't know what Jesus knew about his own soul, he didn't understand what he forfeited for some temporary pieces of silver.

Take some time

- *Reflect*: On the Galatians 4:9 passage and think of what God knows about you.

- *Request*: For God to give you a deeper knowledge of Him and your own heart through the Scriptures.

- *Respond*: As you go about your day, live out the understanding that God knows you to your core and He still loves you. What fruit should that produce in your life?

DAY 2

JUDAS
saw Jesus

'For what can be known about God is plain to them,
because God has shown it to them' (Rom. 1:19).

Jesus' physical appearance is, perhaps, one of the most intriguing aspects of His incarnation. I mean, what did He look like? There are aspects we do know. For starters, He was a male. He was Middle Eastern. But it's hard to get too far past that. Especially when the Scriptures are clear about being unclear about His appearance – other than the fact that he doesn't look like the 'male model' many of the modern-day images depict (Isa. 53:2).

God's sovereign authorship through human authors made sure to leave out physical characteristics of Christ. He even warned against image-worship in the Ten Commandments.

However, Judas Iscariot looked Jesus Christ – the Son of Man, the Second Person of the Trinity, the only One who was fully-God and fully-man – right in the eyes. Let that sink in.

Judas physically saw the One the entire Old Testament prophesied of. He saw the Creator of the universe create a meal for thousands out of a few fish and loaves. He saw Jesus! Some today may deny Jesus and that may seem easier for us to understand. I mean, Jesus has been enthroned for a couple of thousand years at God's right hand, so they've never actually *seen* Him. Judas, however, saw Jesus, so there was no denying His existence.

Seeing is believing?

What's baffling to me is that there are people who still deny mankind's landing on the moon. Even though we have video evidence, they insist it's something manufactured.

Mankind landing on the moon and Judas looking in the face of his Creator prove to us that seeing is *not* always believing. Just because one witnesses something, or has physical proof, doesn't always translate into belief.

The Romans 1 passage cited at the opening of this section also illustrates unbelief in the face of sight. God, in His infinite wisdom and grace, chose to reveal Himself through creation and His Word.

God shows Himself to us through the sun, moon, stars, animal kingdom – in fact anything that's created. More significantly God shows Himself to us through His Word. Therefore, even though we can't claim to see Jesus in the manner in which Judas saw Jesus, we can still see Jesus today.

We see Jesus through all of creation, '*For by him all things were created, in heaven and on earth, visible and invisible, whether thrones or dominions or rulers or authorities—all things were created through him and for him.'* (Col. 1:16). Not only that, but, '*... we have the prophetic word more fully confirmed, to which you will do well to pay attention as to a lamp shining in a dark place ...'* (2 Pet. 1:19a).

Once again, most people assume that their faith would be bolstered if they could just see Jesus. As tempting as that may sound – to actually see the Son of God – we have ample proof that it just isn't a sure-fire plan for faith. Judas, among many many others, saw Jesus and that did not translate to faith.

Sadly, in Christian communities the Word of God just isn't enough for us. We want something more (even a devotional) that can make us sense Jesus on a deeper level. While aids to use alongside Scripture are exactly that – aids – they can never replace the *prophetic Word* God has preserved for us in the Old and New Testaments.

And, while we long one day to see our beautiful Savior, we can affirm what God's Word proclaims: '*Though you have not seen him, you love him. Though you do not now see him, you believe in him and rejoice with joy that is inexpressible and filled with glory, obtaining the outcome of your faith, the salvation of your souls.'* (1 Pet. 1:8-9) In the case of the Christian, not seeing is believing.

Take some time

- *Reflect:* As stated above, Christians far too often fail to see the relevance of God's Word in their daily lives. What do you find yourself looking to most often?

- *Request:* Ask God to help you see Jesus in His Word. Ask that the Holy Spirit would help you to treasure the Bible above any earthly treasure.

- *Respond:* As you go about your day, look to creation as God's general revelation of Himself. On your daily commute, a stroll through the park, or sitting in your backyard, notice the many ways in which you can see God.

DAY 3

JUDAS
felt Jesus

… 'Put your finger here, and see my hands; and put out your
hand, and place it in my side. Do not disbelieve,
but believe' (John 20:27).

Not too long ago a smart-phone app named *Cuddlr* was
created. It is an app designed to allow people to cuddle with
other people (I'm not making this up!). You can sign up for
the app and find fellow 'cuddlees' in your area who also are
longing to physically connect with someone else. As you
may have guessed, this is done with complete strangers. As
weird as it may be to ask one of your friends if they would
cuddle with you, imagine asking a complete stranger.

Understandably the Cuddlr app has drawn much criti-
cism. People are concerned about safety and undiscerning
users of the app finding themselves in a dangerous situation.

However, those concerns didn't seem to stop the app from going viral and being featured in well-known magazines and newspapers.

Now, the popularity of the app is partially due to its absurdity. But part of its popularity is due to the significance of physical touch. People long for physical human inter-action. Children long for parents to hug them, kiss them, or simply to be able to sit in their lap. Husbands and wives must experience hand-holding and sexual intimacy because of God's design of our sexual natures. Touch is important.

Feet washing

I've never had my feet washed. Just to clarify, I have washed my feet but in my adult years my feet haven't felt any other hands than my own. If yours are like mine, feet aren't all that attractive. I understand that some people have cuter feet than others, but … they're still feet.

Well, just imagine Bible times. Dry, crusty, calloused, smelly, dirty, feet. That being so, it didn't seem to slow our Savior down. Out of His overflowing love Jesus purposed to wash the appalling feet of those who would soon use those feet to disassociate themselves with their Savior.

As Judas approached his turn, what was going on in his heart? It had already become hardened towards Jesus. Even still, I wonder how the event was interpreted. Judas felt Jesus' warm hands pour cool water on his dry, wearied feet. Without a doubt, feet in Bible times were accustomed to walking many miles. Therefore, the refreshing water dripping on well-worn feet must have brought relief. Not only that, but Jesus scrubbed the dirt and filth caked on by the many miles.

Judas was looking at the God-man, felt the cool water, witnessed Him gently take his feet in His hands and clean what was once filthy. Judas had surely felt the touch of Christ before in his life, but the significance of this touch would certainly rise to the top.

How do you feel?

It's interesting how we interpret the above question. We associate feeling with touch, but when we're angry, happy or sad we talk about how we *feel*. Feeling, in that case, has little to do with touch. *I just feel unwanted. I feel so confused. I don't know how I'm feeling.*

Maybe this is why people often say they want to *feel* the presence of God. It may be that in this moment, people aren't necessarily hoping to feel some sort of physical touch from God, but sense that He is with them. I believe this is often the case when we are around those we are closest to. For instance, if we experience the loss of a loved one, we often seek the embrace of another. Whether it's a family member or friends, we sometimes don't want words of comfort, rather, we long for the assurance of another's presence by their touch.

This side of heaven, none of us will feel the risen Savior's hand lower our feet into a bowl of water. We won't feel His embrace in those moments of trial. However, in terms of our emotional *feelings* Christ has spoken truth in the midst of confusion. While we can all affirm the importance of physical touch, clarity in the midst of clouded feelings is something invaluable.

What did Judas feel?

Well, we know Judas literally felt the touch of King Jesus. However, in terms of Judas' emotions, he never *felt* the assurance of Christ's claim to be the Anointed One. Judas felt a deeper draw towards unbelief.

The sobering reality is that many of us have felt that way too. This, as you know, is part of the reason this book is being written. What separates us from Judas? There is a fine line between doubt and unbelief. Judas felt the latter. I'm sure he had moments of curiosity towards belief in Jesus, but the doubts continued to be fed until it birthed unbelief.

The cleansing blood of Jesus is powerful enough to cleanse your doubts, but doubts still hold on to belief. If you are one who doubts, cling to the promises of God's Word. While you may not feel Jesus' touch or feel all that certain of what you believe at times, cleave to the promise that you **will** one day feel His hand wiping away every tear (Rev. 21:4).

Take some time

- *Reflect:* What promise do you find yourself clinging to most often? What promise do you find yourself struggling to believe?

- *Request:* Ask God to help your unbelief. Ask Him to birth a deeper trust in His promises.

- *Respond:* Live confidently, today, in the finished work of King Jesus. If you know of friends and family struggling with doubt, assist them by speaking truth.

DAY 4

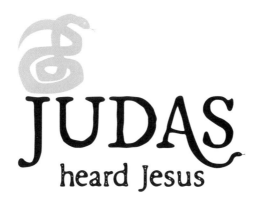

JUDAS
heard Jesus

'You have heard that it was said, **but I say** …'
– Jesus (for example Matt. 5:27).

Benjamin Franklin once said, 'Believe none of what you hear, and only half of what you see.' From this many could conclude that Franklin was a bit of a skeptic. Others may say he was simply exercising discernment. I could see both. After all, we hear a lot of things don't we? When it comes to politics, one side says one thing and the other side says the exact opposite. How are we to believe what we hear?

When it comes to the entertainment industry we hear a whole lot about the lifestyles of the rich and famous. *She broke up with him. That couple is expecting a baby.* Should we believe what we hear? After all, another word for gossip is hearsay. One wonders if an etymological study of hearsay would fine heresy at its root?

What did Judas hear?

One thing we know about Jesus is that He was a master teacher. Erroneously, some today believe that was all Jesus was. While He was more than simply a teacher, He taught with authority. In fact, His style of teaching was so shocking to the religious elite that they pursued His execution.

All of that to say, Jesus was not a boring orator. And, more often than not, Judas had a front-row seat to hear Jesus' teaching. Judas heard Jesus read from the Law. Judas heard Jesus read from the Prophets. Judas heard Jesus reason, explain, exhort, confront, and proclaim the truth that Jesus is *the* way, *the* truth, and *the* light (John 14:6).

Christians rightly place great emphasis on the preaching and teaching of God's Word. It is, after all, the power to make one wise for salvation (2 Tim. 3:15). For the Word of God works in tandem with the Spirit of God.

However, how does the life of Judas give us confidence in that? Judas heard the most gifted Bible teacher to ever walk the face of the earth proclaim, without error or fault, the very Scriptures that testified about Him. There will never be a more gifted orator or theologian handle the Word of God, so what hope do we have?

Hearing with new ears

The church today has been blessed in so many ways. One of those ways is the seemingly infinite access we have to biblical resources. Every book of the Bible is available in more languages than ever. We can access those books of the Bible at the push of a button on our computers and phones. Entire commentaries, endless sermons, podcasts, blogs, etcetera … etcetera … etcetera … have been graciously given to the church of today. As the church of yesteryears utilized the modern advancements of the Guttenberg Press, the church of today has made similar use of the Internet.

However, the church of today finds itself in a similar situation to that of Judas Iscariot. While none of us have a literal front-row seat at the Savior's feet, we have something just as good. Just as good?!? Listen to the apostle Peter:

> For we did not follow cleverly devised myths when we made known to you the power and coming of our Lord Jesus Christ, but we were eyewitnesses of his majesty. For when he received honor and glory from God the Father, and the voice was borne to him by the Majestic Glory, 'This is my beloved Son, with whom I am well pleased,' we ourselves heard this very voice borne from heaven, for we were with him on the holy mountain. And we have the prophetic word more fully confirmed, to which you will do well to pay attention as to a lamp shining in a dark place, until the day dawns and the morning star rises in your hearts, knowing this first of all, that no prophecy of Scripture comes from someone's own interpretation. For no prophecy was ever produced by the will of man, but men spoke from God as they were carried along by the Holy Spirit. (2 Pet. 1:16-21)

This is how I can say we have something just as good. Yes, Jesus Christ in the flesh will be a glorious sight beyond our imaginings, but we have access to the same Word He preached. In fact, as we read above, we hear the very words of God when Scripture is read from. Does God still speak today? Yes! He speaks to us through the Holy Bible. Therefore, each of us should receive great confidence and encouragement from this glorious truth.

Charles Spurgeon, in speaking of a fellow orator said, 'He may preach the gospel better than me, but he cannot preach a better gospel.' In a similar vein, we have access to the same Word, the same gospel, as Judas. While we don't get to hear a more gifted teacher, we have the very words of that teacher recorded for us. Praise God for preserving His Word for all of us to *hear*.

Take some time

- *Reflect:* Do you really believe the Bible is the very Word of God? Do you have confidence that it is how God speaks today?

- *Request:* Ask God to give you great confidence in His recorded Word. Pray that He will help you see the treasure it is.

- *Respond:* Open up His Word now and marvel at the treasure in your hands.

DAY 5

JUDAS
sacrificed for Jesus' Name

'But when you give to the needy, do not let your left hand know what your right hand is doing' (Matt. 6:3).

Our world is obsessed with celebrities, isn't it? Whether it's athletes, movie stars, or some political figure, the world wants to know what is going on in their lives – everything from the mundane to the significant.

And because of this, we are sometimes told about these celebrities' finances. We are told about their paycheck for a movie or how much their contract for the season is. Often we hear about the cost of their vacations or how much they spend on shoes. Truth be told, we're privy to information that's really none of our business.

Not too long ago some celebrities decided to live on just two dollars a day. They did this to make a statement about world poverty. You see, much of the world lives on just two dollars a day. Humbling, isn't it?

I think it can be a good thing to make sacrifices like this. The Lord can teach us much by going with less. However, why did these celebrities make this sacrifice? Was it really to raise awareness for poverty? Was it to increase their image to the public? Was it to try and appear humble? The truth is, I have no idea and there is no way I can judge the intention of their hearts. However, we can say that it is possible to make sacrifices for the wrong reasons.

As we continue to consider the life of Judas, we know he made plenty of sacrifices for Jesus. He left everything he had to follow Him. We know serving Jesus required leaving much of the common conveniences of life. Consider the instructions Jesus gave to the twelve as He sent them out:

> 'You received without paying; give without pay. Acquire no gold or silver or copper for your belts, no bag for your journey, or two tunics or sandals or a staff, for the laborer deserves his food. And whatever town or village you enter, find out who is worthy in it and stay there until you depart.' (Matt. 10: 8b-11)

No money, no bag, leave with whatever is on your backs and trust for God to provide. I would expect that many of us would hesitate at a sacrifice of this magnitude. We like our daily conveniences. We like the clothing we've acquired in our closets. We like our warm beds and full pantries. But Judas left all of this behind for Jesus.

It is a very sobering reality to me that Judas made more material sacrifices for Jesus than I have. I haven't traveled around, leaving much of anything behind, for the sake of His name. What money have I forfeited? What daily comforts – food, water, clothing – have I laid to the side to spread the name of Jesus? And if Judas did these things and still went to hell, what assurance can I have of going to heaven?

Once I was having a conversation with a campus minister in college and we were talking about a similar issue. I was struggling over my minimal sacrifice for Jesus, and the minister asked me, 'What would you need to sacrifice for Jesus to be satisfied?' I replied, 'My life ... and then some.' Meaning, even if I did lay my life down for Jesus, it still wouldn't be enough. I would need to give more than my life to make myself 'right' before God.

The truth is, you or I can never sacrifice enough for God. You can never give enough money, abstain from enough comforts and pleasures in life, to make God happy. What you can do is rely on the sacrifice of Another. What you can believe is that One did make a sacrifice that was great enough for God to look at you and love you. There is nothing you can do today, tomorrow, or for the rest of your life, that can make God the Father more pleased with you than He already is.

The apostle Paul tells us, 'For you know the grace of our Lord Jesus Christ, that though he was rich, yet for your sake he became poor, so that you by his poverty might become rich' (2 Cor. 8:9).

When I told my campus minister that I would have to sacrifice more than my life, I was right. But, Someone else gave a life that is worth much more than I could ever give. Jesus Christ left riches our minds cannot understand. He was enthroned in a place of no sadness, sickness, or suffering, and He left all of that for you.

Celebrities may make many great sacrifices for the wrong reasons. Judas made many big sacrifices, but we know they were for the wrong reasons. You may make sacrifices, but you make them out of a love for the greatest sacrifice that was ever made. You do not make a sacrifice to get right with God. You do not lay your money, your time, your possessions to the side to keep God happy with you. You live your life sacrificially, because Jesus sacrificially lived for you.

Take some time

- *Reflect:* It is true that Jesus has done all the sacrificing that is required for you to enter heaven. However, we sometimes try to live in a way to earn favor with God by our sacrifices. Reflect on ways you try to make yourself right before God and rest in the truth that the only sacrifice has already been made.

- *Request:* In light of the truth that Jesus sacrificed all for you, what are some sacrifices you can make out of love for what He has accomplished? Ask God to show you ways in which you can sacrifice time and money to make Him known.

- *Respond:* Live life sacrificially for others today. Lay your own wants and desires to the side to share the love of Jesus with those you come into contact with. As you do, think of what Jesus laid aside for you and give Him thanks.

DAY 6

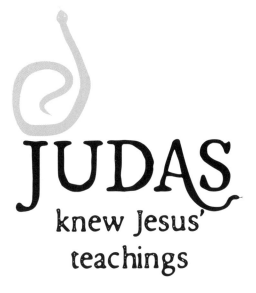

JUDAS
knew Jesus' teachings

'Truly, truly, I say to you, whoever hears my word and believes
him who sent me has eternal life. He does not come into
judgment, but has passed from death to life' (John 5:24).

Every one of us has struggled with listening, whether that's
actually hearing what our bosses have told us to do, intently
listening to the details of a story told by our spouse, or day-
dreaming as we sit in church (at least I've heard of other
people that do that). And I'm sure each of us has received
a bad grade on a test. I have made some pretty bad grades
in my day. It's kind of strange to think that I could listen to
a teacher's lecture, study the material and still make a bad
grade.

As mentioned earlier, Jesus was a gifted teacher. Yes,
people came around Jesus to watch Him perform miracles,

but they also gathered to listen to Him teach (Luke 5:15). He taught with an authority that was unlike others of His time (Matt. 7:29). Multitudes would come from all over to hear Him teach. And we know that, at least sometimes, Judas was right there at His feet. If people would come from all over just to hear Jesus teach, I'm sure His teaching intrigued Judas. I'm sure Judas didn't sit at the feet of Jesus' teachings and merely pretend to be listening – like me in my school classes.

Speaking of my schooling, one thing age can teach you is how much you've forgotten. My geography, for example, is terrible. There was one point in my life when I could identify a good portion of the world map. Now I would be embarrassed if anyone gave me a pop quiz on it. What about the human skeletal system? I remember drawing a diagram, labeling every bone, and acing a test on that material, but not anymore. Geometry and trigonometry used to be two of my best subjects, but I couldn't do either one of those today even if my life depended on it.

Maybe you're old enough to say this is true in your own life. Maybe you had to read a book for a test and now you couldn't even remember what the book was about. Or perhaps it's a subject you once knew but now it's a bit fuzzy.

You see, we learn things and we forget things, but Jesus' teachings were more than something we memorize and regurgitate for a test. Judas was familiar with what Jesus passionately taught about. Even those who opposed Jesus were interested in what He had to say, so we know Judas was most likely captivated by Jesus' authority in teaching. Judas also knew Jesus' teachings well enough to proclaim them to others (more on this in Chapter 12).

Here's a question for you: how well do you know Jesus' teachings? Would you be able to give me a Scripture reference that supports the inerrancy of Scripture? Can you name the twelve disciples? The ten plagues? What about the tribes of Israel? If someone denied the biblical teaching of the trinity, could you turn to Scripture in support of it? What about refuting homosexuality? Abortion? Or other hot button issues? How well do you know the teachings of Scripture?

It is at this point that we must be careful. If we get into the habit of memorizing facts about Scripture or seeing the Bible as nothing more than something to master for trivia, then we can miss the message of Scripture. We also can become prideful to such a degree that our heads won't fit in the door. Maybe a similar mistake is what took place in Judas' heart.

It is one thing for us to hear Jesus' teachings (as we discussed in chapter 4), but it's another thing to believe in the teachings of Jesus. Jesus didn't just teach facts – even though everything He said was factual, His teachings required belief. Belief He expected you to base your life on. Belief that would shape the way you viewed the entire world. Belief that would serve as a foundation for all of life. Belief that results in action. Belief that ruled your life.

You see, Judas' belief in Jesus and His teachings didn't rule his life. Judas may have agreed that Jesus taught with authority, but the authority of those teachings did not possess authority in Judas' life. What I mean is simply this: Judas obviously had other things that were the authority of his life.

Is Jesus the authority of your life? Do you believe in His teachings? Do you notice any change in the way you are living your life?

Take some time

- *Reflect:* If you truly believe in the teachings of Jesus and you call Him your Lord, what fruit do you see in your life as evidence of this? (Remember, you are not saved by your fruit, but fruit points to an inner working of the Spirit.)

- *Request:* Ask the Holy Spirit to strengthen your belief in King Jesus. Your prayer can be similar to the story of the father seeking help for his son, 'I believe; help my unbelief!' (Mark 9:24b)

- *Respond:* Prayerfully live in a way that reflects the Lordship of Jesus Christ. For example, Jesus bled and died on the cross for you; therefore, He owns your time, your money, your possessions. Think of how you can use those for His glory, since they belong to Him.

DAY 7

JUDAS
worshiped
with Jesus

'And as was [Jesus'] custom, he went to the synagogue on the Sabbath day...' (Luke 4:16).

Human beings are designed for relationship. Believers and unbelievers alike are created to be *with* other people. Theologically speaking, this is because we are created in the image of a triune God. Being created in the image of God – Father, Son, and Holy Spirit – makes us, His image-bearers, long for community because their Creator is in perfect community with Himself. This is what makes shared experiences so significant.

Have you ever been to a sporting event? Viewed a movie with a packed house? Been to a concert? Yes, those events are significant in and of themselves, but experiencing them in community makes them much more powerful. You laugh together, you cheer together, your emotions rise in unison as something familiar is sung. Community puts the exclamation point on these events.

Worship is the same way. For the past several years I have been blessed to attend The Gospel Coalition and Together for the Gospel conferences. They are significant moments every year for me. Listening to excellent preaching is a deep blessing. Hearing thousands of voices singing in one accord is a balm to the soul. But, experiencing preaching and singing *with* fellow brothers and sisters is a taste of heaven. It gives my finite mind a tiny glimpse of the eternal.

Worship

The truth is, human beings do not simply worship on Sundays in a church. Worship is not something that takes place in a particular building on a particular day of the week. Worship takes place at a sporting event, worship takes place at a movie theater, a concert, a conference. Worship never stops.

Once again, being created in the image of God means we are created as worshipers. We are created to worship God, but our sin redirects our worship to everything else. We end up worshiping creation over the Creator (Rom. 1:25). This is called idolatry.

To be sure, there's a sense in which we can worship God through creation. That is, we can rightly worship God through a concert, through a sporting event, through enjoying creation like good food or drink. However, our hearts are prone to idolatry because of our sin. Therefore, human beings rarely experience true worship unhindered by their sin of idolatry.

Jesus' custom

Looking at the opening Scripture we read that Jesus' customary practice was to be in the synagogue on the Sabbath. It was His pattern to be there praising God by reading, teaching, and singing to the God of all creation.

Because Jesus was perfection incarnate, His worship was pure. Never did His mind move towards distraction when focus was to be given. Never did thoughts of arrogance about His own teaching rob God the Father of true worship. Never did Jesus give any vain thought to His delivery before a crowd. Jesus worshiped God with all His heart, soul, mind and strength.

Without a doubt, Jesus also worshiped God every day in between Sabbaths. Jesus worshiped God through a good meal, fellowship and a beautiful sunset. He gave thanks to God for a refreshing nap, a glass of water on a hot day and shade from the sun. Jesus' heart was others-minded when it came to service, but theocentric when it came to worship.

Judas' heart

I don't know Judas personally, so I don't know what he was thinking when he worshiped alongside Jesus. But, one thing I do know is that Judas' heart is just like mine. Fallen. It's prone to worship anything other than God. It's prone to forget the God I love. The God who's lavished love on me.

We can be confident that Judas sat and heard Jesus read from the Old Testament. We know that he sang from the Psalms. If it was Jesus' custom to attend public worship in the synagogues, we can be pretty confident that His disciples were with Him, Judas included.

Our worship

Worship is a touchy subject for any Christian with a heartbeat. They debate over styles of singing. What time to worship. What to wear in worship. How long we should worship. The list goes on and on. What's sad is the amount of churches that split over these issues and the lack of love and grace brothers and sisters give to each other on these issues.

While these are all valid concerns and worship is something Christians must give prayer and thought to, can we ever worship like Judas was able to? Judas heard the Savior of the world read Scripture. Judas heard Jesus Christ carry a tune. Judas listened to Jesus expound Scripture. As we've said, Judas heard the One the Scriptures testified about teach from them and still wasn't saved.

Our worship this side of heaven is always going to be flawed. Preachers may preach too long and preach for selfish reasons. Choirs and musicians will play off-key and long for your worship to be directed at them. Congregants will enter sanctuaries with prayerless hearts simply seeking to get something out of worship rather than showing up to worship God.

This doesn't mean we simply shrug our shoulders and try to do our best. Not at all. Jesus offered perfection in worship and He still had lost people in His 'congregation'. We will never find the right formula and nail it each week. We'll never have hearts that rightly worship Creator over creation. But, the One whom all things were created through and for (Col. 1:16), came into His creation. He took our puny worship on Himself while being nailed to the cross. The guilt of our lazy prayers, heartless singing and shallow sermons were reconciled upon His tongue as He asked for His children's forgiveness. All the division our views on worship continue to cause has found unity in the cross. This is something Judas never embraced. Truth be told, this is something many so-called followers of Christ never embrace. Let us have humble hearts toward worship and look to the only One who ever perfectly worshiped.

Take some time

- *Reflect:* Look at what you spend time and money on as well as what makes you angry, in order to uncover your idols. Also, what is your attitude towards corporate worship? Do you sing the songs? Do you listen to the sermons? Do you even get up and go?

- *Request:* Ask God to reveal your idols and call upon the Spirit to help you destroy them. Ask that God would give you a heart that strives for unity in corporate worship.

- *Respond:* Give thanks to God throughout the day as you enjoy His creation. Thank your pastors and musicians for the worship they lead. Pray for your heart and those leading as you approach your next time of corporate worship.

DAY 8

JUDAS
was with Jesus

'And as [Jesus] was leaving Jericho **with** his disciples ...'
(Mark 10:46a).

It should go without saying that Judas was with Jesus.
After all, Judas was a disciple, also known as a follower,
and followers are always behind a leader. To be a faithful
disciple and follower, they had to be with Jesus. Now this
doesn't mean they never left His side. We know Jesus sent
His disciples out on a couple of occasions (Matt. 10:5 and
Luke 10:1). However, they were with Jesus more than
anyone else and they were with Him at intimate moments.

Who are you with?
One time in high school I was visiting a frat house at a

college in my state. (A fraternity is basically a college club and each club has a 'frat' house where many of the members live. Relax, this story is PG). On this particular night at this particular house, they were being a bit selective on who could come in. Before we jump to judgment, there was a well-known band at this house and there was limited room, therefore not everyone could come in.

As I approached the house and entered into a mob of people I began to think, *How am I going to get in?* As I made my way through the mob and closer to the front door, I realized that one of my friends was at the entrance. This guy was a senior and he was informing the mob on who could come in and who could not. As the mob looked at him helplessly, I shouted his name out from amidst the crowd. His eyes met with mine, a smile of recognition came upon his face and he said, *'He's with me.'* I gave the crowd a nod and proceeded in. I felt important. It was a good feeling.

I was able to enter into this private party because of who I was *with*. My attachment to this friend granted me passage into acceptance. People wished they could enter as I passed them by ... this isn't a good story. People were excluded from fellowship and pride was oozing out of my heart. But, who you are with often matters.

You're with Him?!

If we are honest about many of our acquaintances and friendships, they are often selfish. Looking at the above story, I simply used a guy to get into a party. We weren't even that close, but it worked.

Likewise, survey your relationships. What do they tell you? When you look at who your best friends are or who you spend the most time with, I bet you find some selfish reasons. *I like them because they make me laugh. She's my best friend, because she always makes me feel good about myself.* Who's at the center in these examples? Maybe you even have friends who can give you things. Things like a free weekend at a beach house or free tickets to the game. If we're truthful, our relationships often keep us at the center.

One time in high school, I attempted to be selfless in a relationship. There was a particular guy in our high school who had almost no friends. People mocked the way he talked and acted. However, another friend of mine and I realized that we kind of liked this guy. We thought he was funny, so we decided to invite him to hang out with us one weekend. I remember picking him up at his house. His whole family seemed to be shocked that he actually had plans for the weekend, it was obviously a rarity.

The three of us went and grabbed a bite to eat, saw a movie and had a fun Friday night. It was great ... until Monday. Word got out around school that my friend and I hung out with this guy over the weekend. The cafeteria that day was brutal. People laughed at us, they made fun of us. It was humiliating. So, my friend and I did what you think we would; we hardly talked to that guy again. We didn't hang out with him anymore. We made one thing clear: we were not with that guy! It grieves my heart today. Throughout the years we did mature a bit and come to be friendly with that guy, and even include him. But, we were so unloving.

Who's with whom?
Towards the end of Judas' life he was only with Jesus to deliver Him over to be crucified. Even though there may have been somewhat innocent intentions early on to be with Jesus, those changed to selfish gain. Judas used Jesus like

many of us use our relationships. After all, Jesus claimed to be the Chosen One and King; therefore, maybe Judas thought Jesus would be his ticket to fame and fortune? Judas was only with Jesus to get something from Him. But don't you often do the same thing?

Judas ended up being ashamed of and disinterested in Jesus. In reality, why would Jesus be interested in being *with* anyone other than His Father and the Spirit? Why would Jesus want to leave perfect unity to dwell in disunity? Why would Jesus want to leave the embrace of His Father to feel the fist of a Roman soldier? Why would Jesus want to claim that He's with the disciples when He knows they will leave Him in His hour of need? Why?

What Judas didn't realize was that he was with the One who would wipe away every tear. He was with the One who would make all things new. He was with the One who took on poverty to purchase a lifetime of riches for those who followed Him. While Christians may be quick to say, *I'm with Jesus!,* by grace, Jesus says, *I'm with you. You are mine. And, no one can snatch you away* (John 10:28-30).

Take some time

- *Reflect:* Survey your relationships and see how your selfishness can manifest itself. See those who you're afraid to be seen with. Notice those you hold to a higher standard and hope you're seen with.

- *Request:* Ask the Spirit to change your heart in your relationships. Ask for a selfless heart towards others. Ask God to take away a heart of favoritism and replace it with love.

- *Respond:* Love the unlovable and lesser in your midst. Be reminded that you were the difficult one Jesus reached out and loved.

DAY 9

JUDAS
witnessed
Jesus' miracles

'There is a boy here who has five barley loaves and two fish,
but what are they for so many?' (John 6:9).

As I was nearing graduation from college, I was able to
ride along and job-shadow a man I had great respect for.
He was an elder in the church I was attending and had a
great family that he seemed to faithfully disciple, so I was
interested in learning about his particular job, but I was also
excited to get to spend some time with him.

Throughout the day we talked about various things: his
family, my plans for the future, specifics about his job. At
one point in the day he began to talk about his son's soccer
team. What struck me was all the work the father was
putting into this club. He was at meetings, making phone

calls, arranging volunteers, assisting in carpooling, teaching the son fundamentals, spending money on cleats, socks, shin-guards, meals on the road and gas, just to name a few.

After he continued to talk about his involvement, I replied, 'Wow. It's crazy to think of all the work you're putting into this and your son doesn't even know it.' I'll never forget his reply, 'I don't do it so he'll acknowledge how hard I'm working. I do it because I love him.' All the phone calls, meetings, money weren't simply this father showing love to his son. The focus wasn't all the work. The focus wasn't the time sacrificed. The reason was a father's love for his son. Love was the focus.

Isn't that amazing!?

Water into wine. Calming of the storm. The blind have sight, the lame walk, the deaf hear ... amazing! These are the stories we all hear growing up, and Judas had a front row seat to witness them.

Many people think, *If my unbelieving spouse could have seen Jesus heal the leper, surely she'd believe.* We often have these thoughts, don't we? Whether it's an unbelieving family member or close friend, we assume a close-up encounter with Jesus would surely move them from faithlessness to faith. We're positive the supernatural amazement of it all would soften their hard heart. Even though we know it didn't work for thousands in Jesus' day, for some reason we think it would work for the people of today.

Judas was there. He began to pick up basket after basket of fish and bread. Prior to this excess he was discussing with the others: *It's almost supper time. These people are going to be hungry. We better send them in to the markets before they close. We don't have enough money or food for this many mouths.* And then he witnesses a young boy present all the food he had to them.

As Judas' eyes surveyed the five loaves and two fish, he knew that would barely feed Jesus and the disciples. Yet, he walked over to Jesus after He looked up to heaven, gave thanks, and broke the bread. He was puzzled that he was able to continue to deliver fish and bread to the seated crowd. How was he continually going back to Jesus to fill up his basket? How were the crowds continually able to reach into the basket and not come up empty-handed? Hands were reaching out for what was once two fish and receiving plenty. There was no want among the crowd; they all received. In fact, we are told there was such a surplus of food, the disciples actually had to pick up extra – our God gives more than we could ask or imagine.

The disciples began with confusion over how they would provide for thousands and ended in bewilderment over their excess. Little did they know that their confusion over how they would provide for these people was the beginning of another miracle. Their despair over a lack of food leads to blindness over the fact that they were in the presence of the Bread of Life.

Why are we surprised?
But how … how did Judas witness all this and still miss out on the Bread of Life? How did he witness miracle after miracle and not believe Jesus was the Son of God? If we look at this from another perspective it might help us to see how Judas could have caught the miracle, but missed out on salvation.

Have you ever heard of the term *fair-weather fan*? It references those fans of certain sports teams who are loyal to their team as long as their team is performing well. You'll see them dressed up, face painted and cheering loud when their team is dominating all the other opponents. However, as soon as the team begins to see a decline in the win column and an increase in the loss column, their attire is different, the face paint comes off and the cheers diminish.

Judas could be compared to a fair-weather fan. If Judas followed Jesus from the beginning and he saw no miracles, witnessed no fanfare from crowds, and didn't have the sense that he was a body-guard for a celebrity, he probably would have been a little less loyal. But Judas was with a super-star. He was with this man who was being talked about all over the region.

Think about it, how much faith does one have to employ when witnessing a miracle? Judas was seeing all of these amazing acts, which should make faith less of an exercise for him. Just as a fan doesn't struggle to follow the team when they're performing at a high level, Judas didn't struggle to follow Jesus when he saw miracle after miracle being performed.

The greatest miracle of all?

We may think that Judas had a better opportunity to believe because he was with Jesus during these miracles, but there's a real sense that this was a disadvantage. For starters, we are confident that Judas wasn't a true follower of Christ, so his witnessing of these miracles didn't lead to his conversion. That much is obvious. What we need to realize is the fact that Judas must have been more enamored with the miracle than the One who performed them. In a sense, the miracles distracted him from the Miraculous Man, which makes his witnessing of these miracles a disadvantage.

While many who are much smarter than I may give reason to disagree, I think the incarnation is the greatest miracle of all, because literally it gave birth to every miracle that would follow. Furthermore, it marked what every Old Testament miracle was pointing to. God, taking on flesh, to dwell with sinners in order to ensure those sinners could one day dwell with Him. The fact that murderers, adulterers, rapists, pedophiles, liars, abortion doctors, and fornicators could dwell in eternity with God is a miracle. And all of this is a fact because God added flesh to His glory and walked this earth in the man Christ Jesus.

Judas missed this. Judas, as much as any normal human being, was amazed at the miracles he saw. Any atheist of our day would be amazed by what Jesus did, but they still might not believe. Judas followed a man who was doing amazing things, and that's where it stopped for Judas. He was persuaded to follow Jesus based on His performance, but it never led to his amazement over a man who would walk this earth in order that we might one day walk with Him in eternity.

Judas was too focused on bread to see the Bread of Life.

Take some time

- *Reflect :* Think of the ways you are similar to Judas. Are you fixated on the miracles or the performance of Jesus, and not on the One performing? Are you enamored with the 'stuff' He did, and not His person? Nothing is wrong with a fascination with His accomplishments, but don't let it cloud your mind from him.

- *Request:* Ask God to help you love Him.

- *Respond:* Live in light of the incarnation today. Live in a way that understands that your guilt was taken because Jesus came to bear it on the cross. Live with an understanding that Jesus dwelt with unlovable people, and so love the unlovable in your midst today.

DAY 10

JUDAS
laughed
with Jesus

'Philip found Nathanael and said to him, "We have found him
of whom Moses in the Law and also the prophets wrote, Jesus of
Nazareth, the son of Joseph." Nathanael said to him,
"Can anything good come out of Nazareth?" Philip said to him,
"Come and see." Jesus saw Nathanael coming toward him and said
of him, "Behold, an Israelite indeed, in whom there is no deceit!"
Nathanael said to him, "How do you know me?" Jesus answered
him, "Before Philip called you, when you were under the fig tree,
I saw you"' (John 1:45-48).

I've always thought the above section of Scripture is funny.
Not only do we have Nathanael's sarcastic remark, we
have Jesus 'one-upping' his remark by sharing his vision of
Nathanael under the fig tree. I think the scene is supposed

to be funny and I think it gives us a taste of the sense of humor Jesus had. I'm sure He was funny.

Laughter is a unique blessing from God. Laughter, it is said, fosters longevity of life, decreases stress, keeps marriages healthy and is consistently referred to as 'the best medicine'.

Laughter is especially unique when you consider the fact that we are sinners. God created us perfect, gave us everything we needed and then we rebelled against Him. The blessings could have ended at that point, but God continues to give and give to His rebellious creatures. One of those blessings is laughter, an emotional response that fills us with good feelings to such a degree that we open our mouths and force a sound out.

As we all know, laughter comes in different shapes and sizes. Some people give a loud burst of laughter (shotgun laugh), some give several repeated short bursts (machinegun laugh), and others laugh silently while spinning in circles (?). Whatever your style is, we can all agree that laughter is pleasurable.

Laughter points us to the Garden
One night my wife and I went to listen to a well-known comedian. When we got there, we were happy to discover that we knew several people present in the auditorium. Prior to the performance, people were up walking around sharing conversation, like one big happy family. As the performance began, we were united as one in laughter. We laughed at all the punch lines, clapped at the appropriate times and cheered at the realization of a professional honing his craft. By the end of the night, my face hurt from all the smiling I had done.

Laughter unifies people. One truth I've noticed about laughter is the affirmation that occurs with it. Whenever people laugh in a large crowd – at a movie theater, a comedian's performance, or someone telling a humorous story in the living room – they look at each other when the punch line occurs. People begin to laugh and immediately look to their right, left or behind to affirm their sharing of this experience.

The experience of laughter points us back to the Garden of Eden as well as forward to heaven. Laughter brings unity and unity is a taste of perfection. Unity was displayed in Adam and Eve's perfect unity with God. God promises that every tongue and tribe and nation will be united by the blood of His Son in the new heavens and new earth (Rev. 7:9). Jesus displays the importance of unity in His 'High Priestly Prayer' asking that His followers will be one like He and the Father are one (John 17:22).

Unity is vital to Christianity and laughter is one avenue that gives us unity. It can bring unity about in the young and old, those from different races, and those who were once enemies. Laughter pushes differences aside and ushers in oneness.

Unity or disunity?
With all the time Judas and Jesus spent together, you can rest assured there was laughter. Now, this is complete speculation, but, as I said earlier, I would venture to say that Jesus was a pretty funny guy. For starters, He possessed perfect joy and happiness. Secondly, if He could raise the dead, make the blind see, the deaf hear, and dispel leprosy from the infected, surely He could deliver a joke.

Regardless of Jesus' supposed divine humor, we can be fairly confident that the crew of disciples laughed from time-to-time. Therefore, Judas and Jesus shared this unifying event. This shouldn't be downplayed.

Laughter is a vulnerable and intimate thing. I have already described some of the responses people give from laughter. At its most basic form, people open their mouths and an uncontrollable noise comes out. All the while, they're typically making eye-contact with others in the room. Most people keep emotions private, but laughter exposes something deep inside of us. It shows people our hearts in many ways.

Judas' heart was laid bare before Jesus (in more ways than through laughter). In terms of the humorous, Jesus may have placed His hand on Judas' shoulder as they shared a comical moment. They looked in each other's eyes as an instance sparked an emotional response of hilarity they agreed upon. Judas shared these refreshing, unifying moments with Jesus and he still brushed them to the side for some spare change.

Laughter's limits

Preachers debate about a lot of things, and they should. Any time a man is entering the pulpit to herald God's Word to His people, he should not do so with levity. It is a serious thing to exposit the Holy Scriptures; therefore, debate is needed to determine what is appropriate and inappropriate.

Humor in the pulpit is one of those debated things. I for one, believe that humor can be a vitally important tool in the pulpit (see above). However, I have also been present in sanctuaries where it is abused. I have seen men who simply abuse the good gift of laughter to serve their love of self. I have seen men who have – as far as I could discern, built the entire 'sermon' around their funny story. That is, they haven't opened up God's Word and thought, *What does this say?* Rather, they opened up God's Word and thought, *How can I fit this funny story around this text?*

Humor can be a mighty tool, but it has limits. I think we can confidently say this based on the life of Judas. One would be hard-pressed to assume there was no laughter shared in those intimate moments between Jesus and His disciples. Therefore, we know they shared the unifying experience of laughter, but it wasn't enough to save Judas. Laughter has limits.

Laughter can share our hearts, draw us together, fill us with a euphoric response that borders on ecstasy, but it cannot change a heart of stone into a heart of flesh. This is a truth that needs to resonate with those preaching God's Word, but it needs to resonate with every member of God's church. Have you turned God's church into a social event that serves your emotions? Do you simply like being a part of a church because you share laughs with your small group? Men's breakfast? Women's Bible study? Are you the 'comedian' at your church and the laughter of those present is merely serving your idolatry of self, which isn't testimony to a regenerate heart?

These are questions we all need to ask of ourselves. Laughter is a powerful blessing from God. It is something that can bring about a deep unity. But, undiscerning laughter can blind God's people to the potential danger of their frivolous profession of faith.

Take some time

- *Reflect:* Think of the blessing that laughter is and thank God for it. Think of the ways laughter can be abused. Search your heart: is the laughter you enjoy with brothers and sisters fostering a surface-level unity similar to what Judas and Jesus had? *Do you simply go to church for a humorous, social time or is there a deeper unity present?*

- *Request:* Ask God for discernment in the area of laughter. Ask that you would be vulnerable to God with your humor. Ask that He would expose the hidden idols in this area. Ask that He would remove any blindness fostered by lightheartedness.

- *Respond :* Give praise to God for the laughter we share with friends. Thank Him for this enormous gift that can point our hearts towards eternity. Preachers, be cautious of how you may abuse humor. Parishioners, be cautious of only wanting a sermon that entertains you and makes you laugh.

DAY 11

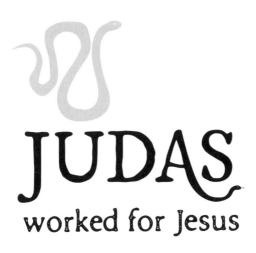

JUDAS
worked for Jesus

"Beware of practicing your righteousness before other people in order to be seen by them, for then you will have no reward from your Father who is in heaven" (Matt. 6:1).

Growing up, I was pretty lazy. I *hated* manual labor. I know hate is a strong word, which is why I'm using it in this context. I abhorred work. I would often work harder to get out of work, probably expending more energy in the process.

On one specific occasion when I was to mow our lawn, I put up a considerable fight. Even though my father's wishes won the day, I wasn't ready to wave the white flag just yet. As my disdain for grass grew under the hot sun in my back yard, I attempted to end this 'injustice' at every possible turn. As my plotting grew, I noticed a possible way out of this chore.

As providence would have it, we owned a particularly old lawn mower. Duct tape held the bag together, wheels were wobbly and the pull-string was almost worn through. That was my opportunity! You see, I could tell that the pull-string was about to give way, so I was sure to work it extra-hard to ensure its life-expectancy wouldn't last another mowing. I pulled and pulled, making sure to rub it a little more against the metal piece that held it in place. Again and again, until … snap! … victory at last! I was finally freed from the taskmaster that day.

I'm sure I went in and put up a believable performance in front of my parents. I'm also sure I convinced my conscience that the rope would have broken soon anyway, attempting to alleviate any guilt I may have had. I can't remember how long the delay fed my aversion towards hard work, but I'm sure it wasn't long.

There's going to be work in heaven?!
By God's grace alone, the idea of hard work and manual labor is something I actually enjoy today. To be honest, there are many times I look forward to it. And I'm happy to say that my parents and I often laugh over how I used to act and how much I've changed in this area. If it weren't for the laughter we share over this, I'd probably feel a little more guilt, but I marvel at God's grace here.

There's something about work that's truly satisfying. Like the aforementioned truth of laughter pointing us to the Garden of Eden, so is the reality of work. One of my favorite aspects of work is the admiration that follows a completed task. After the time, effort and sweat is spent, seeing the completed task brings great joy. This should make us think of our Creator God.

After God had spent six days making *everything*, He stepped back from creation and (get this) admired …

Himself! You see, this would be vain selfishness if it were anyone else, but since God actually created it all and since He's perfectly glorious, He deserves all glory. So when He pauses after the creation account and rests to admire His work, that is right, good and true.

Working for Jesus

As we continue to reflect on Jesus' perfection, we know that He worked perfectly. What is meant by this is the fact that He was never lazy … not once. He never complained when work was to be done, even though He was tired. He always had perfect joy when a job needed assistance and when He saw that task through to its completion.

It would only be right to assume that Jesus' work ethic rubbed off on His disciples, and that they would carry with them a similar, although imperfect, work ethic. Therefore, Judas actually worked hard, right alongside Jesus. If there were widowed and poor around them, and there were, he exerted effort at Jesus' commands as well as His example. When journeys needed to be taken across hot deserts, Judas was trekking for the Kingdom.

Surely Judas had blistered hands, scrapes and bruises, sore feet and achy joints in an effort to serve the Kingdom. We can rest assured this was the case, because we know this was the case with Jesus. We know, in Christ's humanity, that He wore His earthly body out for the sake of His people. For the sake of those in need, those hurting, those who were hopeless, Jesus worked for them. He came not to be served, but to serve (Mark 10:45).

We can be sure that Jesus worked, because work is so ingrained into creation. The first Adam worked, because God created him to do so (Gen. 2:15). Pre-Fall, God wanted the first Adam to work and we know this work wasn't cursed, but a blessing. It was always fulfilling and always joyous. Yet after the first Adam's rebellion, Jesus Christ – the second Adam (Rom. 5:12-21) - came to work and ensure a future eternity of perfectly joyous work for God's people.

Work is ingrained in all of mankind. From the lazy to the 'workaholic', work is in our DNA. There are those who hate it and continue to rebel against it and those who worship work and turn it into an idol that never rests. Both extremes are wrong as both are perverting the gift of rest. Our work is to be done for God's glory and our rest is to be done recognizing that God is at work to keep this earth spinning, not us.

Judas' work ethic was a perversion of what God desires of humanity. Although Judas did appear to be exerting energy for the Kingdom, he was truly exerting energy in the name of the 'kingdom of self.' You see, that ingrained notion to work – that was written on his heart and ours – was only being exerted for self, not service. He wasn't truly working for the Kingdom, he was simply doing something that comes naturally to most of us. Yes he was doing a lot of good things, but doing it from bad motives. Therefore, in the end, all the good he did wasn't good that pleased God.

As Paul tells us in Romans, 'For the mind that is set on the flesh is hostile to God, for it does not submit to God's law; indeed, it cannot. Those who are in the flesh cannot please God' (Rom. 8:7-8). While there are intricacies to discuss in this verse, you can rest assured that those who aren't converted, cannot please God.

All the sweat, time, energy and calluses that Judas worked up didn't amount to anything in eternity. Judas simply worked from the God-given notion he's placed on all of humanity's heart. He didn't work out of thankfulness to God, because his heart was not captured by God. Yet those who are God's children work for the glory of Christ, and this pleases God.

Take some time

- *Reflect:* Think of Jesus' work ethic and be moved in awe over His work. We should be humbled by the diligence and hard work of our Savior and ask for the Spirit's power to work in a similar way.

- *Request:* That God would give you a greater Christ-centered focus on your work. Ask that He would help you to see that all of your work is solely a work of grace. Your work does not save you. Christ's work already saved you. Now, you are saved in order to do work.

- *Respond:* Have joy when you work knowing that it's rooted in creation and you will one day work in a perfect environment. Let this perspective shape the work you do in the job God has currently called you to.

DAY 12

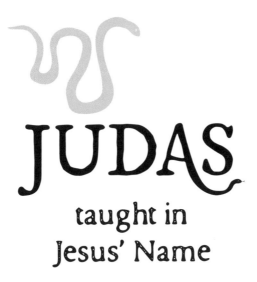

JUDAS

taught in Jesus' Name

'[T]he Lord appointed seventy-two others and sent them on ahead of him, two by two, into every town and place where he himself was about to go … and [Jesus told them to] say to them, "The Kingdom of God has come near to you"' (Luke 10:1, 9).

As I started out in ministry, I wasn't too smart. I do not say this to demean the way that God has created me or to put down any possible gifts He has bestowed upon me. I simply say this intending to communicate that I didn't think things through in terms of what a call to the ministry looked like. Let me explain.

I have a sinful fear of speaking in public. I can say that now I have overcome so much of this fear, only by grace! I often reflect, in wonder, over the ways God has grown me and the contexts in which He has had me speak with great confidence. Glory to Him alone! That being said, when I was starting out, I was petrified to speak in front of other human beings. Yet for some reason I thought I could get through seminary and work at a church, while avoiding any scenario that might call me to speak … you see, not smart.

When I initially started volunteering with the youth ministry I've been working with now for over ten years, I said, 'I'd love to assist in whatever way you need me, except public speaking. I'll be happy to serve, hang out with youth, but I'll never teach/speak.'

That only lasted for a while. Some time later, the senior pastor actually put me on the preaching calendar. When my friend and fellow co-worker informed me of this, my heart-rate increased, my palms began to sweat and terror seized my body. I seriously had a sinking feeling in my stomach and I do not exaggerate when I say this, I was nervous every week leading up to that sermon even though I wasn't scheduled to preach for another several months. When the time finally came for me to preach, I was so nervous that the stress of preaching made me physically ill and I was unable to preach until the following week. Extreme, right?!

A healthy fear

It has been said that public speaking is the number one fear among all people and death is number two. Jerry Seinfeld quips, 'People would rather be in the coffin than giving the eulogy.' While most of our fear of public speaking is motivated out of our idol of self-love, there is some healthy fear when it comes to preaching or teaching in God's name.

It's one thing to give a toast and another thing altogether to open God's Word as His herald. God Himself says so, when He tells us through His servant James that, 'we who teach will be judged with greater strictness' (James 3:1). Therefore, those preaching God's Word would do well to have a godly fear when entering the pulpit. As my preacher always says, 'I still get butterflies when I preach, but now they fly in formation.' In one sense he's communicating that he always needs humility when he's entering the pulpit.

As Jesus sent out the seventy-two there was a certain amount of teaching each of them was commanded to do. They were given a basic gospel-message to communicate, 'The Kingdom of God has come near to you' (Luke 10:9b), and they were prepared for agreement or strife. Christ had prepared them for either outcome. We assume this group engaged in a bit more dialogue depending on their audience. Regardless, there was some type of teaching, explaining or instructing that occurred.

I wonder what Judas thought about this interchange? How vehemently did he communicate the gospel to those who opposed this message? How much joy did he convey when his listeners embraced this idea of God's Kingdom? What was going on in his heart and mind as he spoke eternal truths from a tongue that would later conspire to kill the Savior he proclaimed?

A preacher's confession

Not too long ago I was attending an excellent youth conference. At the beginning of the week they gather all the youth workers together and relay various logistics as well as communicating gospel-centered goals for the week. Those in charge also asked the main speaker to come forward and convey his message and ask for prayers. He said something very candid and profound as he asked for prayers. It was something to this effect: 'I ask that you pray for my heart. Every time I speak I want to do a good job. I want the students to like me. I want the students to hear me. But, I ultimately want them to fall in love with Jesus and not me. However, I know that I have to do a good job and have the students like me in order for them to listen to what I'm saying. There's this inner struggle going on in my heart of wanting to be worshiped, but wanting students to worship Jesus. Pray for my heart.'

This man conveyed a struggle that's present in every preacher's and teacher's heart ... sin! Sin poisons our thoughts and intentions so that we rarely, if ever, do things from pure motives. The truth is, the self-serving teaching Judas did is present in my heart and yours. The doubts Judas had as he conveyed truths about the Kingdom are the same doubts we struggle with. The lack of joy Judas had over gospel-truths is the same lack of joy you have and the same David had when he asked God to restore unto him the joy of salvation (Ps. 51:12).

As it has been noted, the heart of Judas and the hearts of each of us are very similar. Judas doubted; so do we. Judas was selfish; so are we. Judas lacked joy; so do we. Yet one obvious, vital distinction present in Judas' heart was unbelief. Judas was an unbeliever. We're familiar with the phrase 'Practice what you preach'. While preaching and teaching are distinct, they have similarities. When it came to Judas' life, he didn't practice what he taught.

It's one thing to teach about something, but another thing to live it out. Judas may have taught about the Kingdom and even engaged others about the Kingdom, but he never had a heart that embraced the Kingdom and lived it out before others.

Take some time

- *Reflect:* Do you find your heart hardened to the truth you hear taught or the truth you teach? Is your belief sincere in hearing and receiving the gospel from the pulpit? Do you find that the gospel gives you joy in the midst of sorrow?

- *Request:* Ask God that your heart would be softened to accept this truth. Pray that God would give you increasing joy in the light of Christ's finished work. Ask that in the midst of your unbelief, God would give you belief (Mark 9:24).

- *Respond:* Stop doubting the truth of God's Word. Have confidence that Jesus is who He says He is. One practical way to do this is to dispel notions of guilt. Yes Christians need to have guilt and conviction over sin, but we shouldn't wallow in it. Our guilt should move us to the cross and release us from guilt. Wallowing in guilt is a result of pride and a lack of belief. Move away from guilt and have confident belief in Christ's finished work … today!

DAY 13

JUDAS

healed in Jesus' Name

'And he called to him his twelve disciples and gave them authority over unclean spirits, to cast them out, and to heal every disease and every affliction' (Matt. 10:1).

Many of you have seen the amazing YouTube videos of human beings hearing for the first time. In one particular video, it displays a hearing device placed in an infant's ear and him hearing his mother for the first time. After I viewed this, and wiped away all the tears, I marveled at that moment; thanking God for His grace and the ingenuity He bestowed on those who created this life-changing technology.

Imagine if you were the one who invented that device. Imagine placing that device in a child's or adult's ear and they begin to hear noises and sounds that are everyday to us, but completely foreign to them. Could you imagine the joy that would come over you? Could you imagine the sense of value and fulfillment received from the job you had? It would be overwhelming to know you're being used to change so many lives. Similarly, think of the disciples. In the above passage Jesus explicitly gives the ability to fight demonic forces and heal to each of His disciples.

Immediately after this passage Matthew goes on to list the twelve. These were twelve average men who were now performing miracles that were anything but average. Put yourselves in their sandals. What would it have been like to make a blind person see? Imagine walking up to a human with disfigured eyes or eyes that were visibly clouded over and grey, then touching or speaking to them and seeing them restored. Just as many who were moved to tears by the viral videos, the disciples and those witnesses must have been overcome with emotion. How can any human being, believer or not, be emotionless at the highly emotional event of a fellow human being seeing for the first time? The event would be a truly unifying moment.

The blind see, the deaf hear, the mute speak, the bleeding stops, the leprous are cleansed, the possessed are freed, the outcasts are brought in and the crippled leap for joy, all by the hands of ordinary men; through God's work.

Too much power

Power is an interesting thing. No, I'm not talking about electricity, I'm speaking more broadly of power. When I speak of power, I'm speaking of control, influence, authority, rule, clout. The power displayed by the twelve was literally extraordinary.

Most are familiar with the old adage spoken by John Dalberg-Acton, that, 'Absolute power corrupts absolutely.' Lord Acton was very much against those with power and prestige as he thought that most 'Great men are almost always bad men.' He asserts what we so often know is true: power corrupts.

In our day we are accustomed to power in various forms. We may think of the politician who has influence over his constituents. When she or he gets up to give a speech, waves of applause pour forth from every word that rolls off their tongue. The speaker realizes that they have power over their followers.

We may also think of movie stars when we think of power (we have attached the label of 'star' to them after all). Whenever there's a premier for their new movie, crowds descend upon the scene to snap pictures, scream and have a chance to touch the celebrity. The millions of dollars their films make at the box office carry a certain amount of power and affirmation that they are able to wield from time to time. They may even be able to get away with certain things others are not.

Athletes are the same way. They have been gifted with a power unlike others. The athleticism they are able to display is unlike many around them. Therefore, these people end up being worshiped. The fans end up wearing their jersey, asking for their autograph and bowing down in humble allegiance to their team.

Likewise, the disciples and Jesus were celebrities of their day. Just like politicians, movie stars and athletes have people fawning over them, the disciples understandably had people worshiping them. They were changing the lives of their followers in ways empty platitudes from a podium, moving pictures from a screen and homeruns are unable to do. They were recreating people to the way they should have been. They were making the broken whole again. This is a power that, in many regards, deserves celebrity. There are celebrities of our day that are somewhat puzzling as to why they are celebrities, but the disciples' celebrity is understandable.

The poison of power

There are some of us who think that being a celebrity would solve our problems. Conveniences and pleasures that are currently unattainable would be available at our fingertips. However, there is great danger that accompanies power.

The disciples were not above this danger. While centuries separate them from the modern-age celebrity, their hearts were prone to the same sins. Healing those of their sicknesses or ridding their bodies of an evil spirit would move anyone to tears. Each time these people would, without a doubt, bow down to the disciples, have hugged the disciples, offered them money, cheered with uncontrollable joy; and this is understandable to anyone with a heartbeat. But those with a heart of stone would be filtering those encounters in a different manner than others.

You see, a humble heart, while it is still sinful, would share in the joy of those who are made whole. A humble heart would bow with the formerly afflicted and give praise to God. A humbled heart would realize that the gift they just imparted was imparted to them by Another. Simply put, a humble heart wouldn't boast. Power given to a humble heart produces kindness, gentleness and love. It softens all the more.

Power given to a heart of stone, however, produces pride and death. This was the heart of Judas. Judas witnessed the joy of others, the healing of others, the life-altering events that flowed from his fingertips and tongue as he spoke in Jesus' name, but he turned inward. Instead of worshiping the Savior, whose name he healed in, he began in his own heart to worship his own name. He worshiped his own fingertips. Judas could heal others through Jesus' power, but he couldn't heal his own heart.

Take some time

- *Reflect:* Do you notice tendencies in your own heart where you're moved to worship yourself? Think of the Pharisees and their desire to be worshiped by mankind in the market places and places of honor at banquets – what are ways in which you seek to be worshiped by others?

- *Request:* Ask for God to guard you from a heart of pride. Ask God to grant you a heart of humility. Ask God to help you see others as people you can serve, not people who puff up your pride and give you worship.

- *Respond:* Go about your day today thanking God for gifts He's given you. If people are prone to 'worship' you for various gifts, live in a way that points them away from yourself and towards Jesus. Serve others today knowing that Jesus also came not to be served but to serve (Matt. 20:28).

DAY 14

JUDAS
served in Jesus' Name

'And proclaim as you go, saying, "The kingdom of heaven is at hand." Heal the sick, raise the dead, cleanse lepers, cast out demons. You received without paying; give without pay' (Matt. 10:7-8).

Confession time. I have a hard time loving certain celebrities. I understand that, as a Christian, I should not foster feelings of disdain towards other image bearers, but it's hard at times. I need to repent and pray for love towards these people who are, strangely, a part of my life. Oprah Winfrey is one of those that can be a little difficult to love.

Many people worship her, but it seems that her greatest worshiper is herself. She has her own show that typically displays how great she is. She has her own magazine that only ever displays a picture of herself on the cover. She now has her own cable network.

That being said, she has done a lot to serve and care for others. She is the richest woman alive. What's interesting is the fact that her services are typically trumpeted to the entire watching world. Now, I understand that it's hard for any celebrity to do anything that's hidden from a world that's always watching, but it seems that trumpeting her service is something that remains consistent in her life. Whenever she seems to do something good, a camera isn't too far away.

Needy needs

Truth be told, I see a lot of Oprah in me ... you know what I mean? That is, if I do something good, I often want credit for it. It's hard to do something good that no one ever sees. To put forth hard work and get no pat on the back. The Bible calls this service. Service is doing something that's typically hard, typically inconvenient and you typically shouldn't expect anything in return.

Because of mankind's innate sinfulness, we are needy by nature. Not only does our sin make us needy, but we are not autonomous. That is, we were created by God, which makes us simply and profoundly in need. God did not need anything. He didn't even need human beings. God created them after His image to display His glory. We are unnecessary yet meaningful at the same time.[1]

The point is, God has no needs, but we do. Since we are creature and God is Creator, this makes us dependent upon Him for all of our needs. Our rebellion against Him only

---

1. This thought originated from Lincoln Harvey's *A Brief Theology of Sport* (Cascade Books, 2014).

furthers our neediness. Since we are broken creatures, we need others to help us think at times, we need others to help us walk as we age or deal with an injury and we need others to care for us as we enter this world as children. Human beings, by nature, are needy.

Absent of neediness

One mark of Jesus' ministry was service. He left a throne where need was foreign and entered a world of needy people. Prior to that, before the creation of the world, God the Father, Son and Holy Spirit were complete in every way. They are distinct from one another, but fully self-sufficient and whole. There was nothing they needed.

Jesus, however, left a place of completion and entered a world of constant need. He gave and gave and gave from sun up until sun down. He offered Himself over and over again, 'free of charge.'

When Jesus took on flesh He became aware of need. Jesus' earthly body needed water, needed food, needed rest. The One who had utter wholeness took on need to free us from neediness. Jesus' life was marked with service to those who had need.

Judas' need

As I said, our sin causes us to be needy people. Because of this, our service can end up serving our own need. What's intended to turn us outward (service) ends up turning in on self. We often need others to need us, so our selfishness can easily be camouflaged in service. Where Jesus' life was marked with service, Judas' service was marked with self.

It can be a good thing to be needed. It is nice to know that we have worth and value before others. That our thoughts matter to others. That our gifts can help others. That our jokes can make people laugh. It's great to be needed but it can also become idolatrous.

A way this is manifested in our service is when we think certain ministry cannot occur apart from us. We believe we are the ones 'keeping the ship afloat'. If it weren't for our service, the mission would surely fail. The needs of others can end up feeding our ego; our service is solely functioning to serve self.

Just as we mentioned in the previous chapter about power feeding pride, service does the same thing. For Judas, this is surely what it did. Judas' service was not out of a desire to help others, but to help self. The need he saw in others was simply a way to feed his pride. Every person who needed food. Every person who needed shelter. Every person who had a question, a sickness, an affliction was a person who needed him.

Being needed is not a bad thing, but it can become an idolatrous thing when it enters the heart of a sinner like you and me. Judas took something good, like service, and turned it into something damning.

Think back again to the last supper: the disciples were in shock that one of them would betray Jesus. Why? Because service almost always looks selfless to the naked eye. Judas was doing so much for other people. It appeared that he was getting exhausted and sweaty in the name of Jesus, but he was actually getting exhausted and sweaty in the name of Judas.

Take some time

- *Reflect:* Take a look at your service. How much is it feeding your idol of self? How often are you fueled by others' apparent neediness of you? Have you turned the need of others into an idol? Are you even serving for the Lord at all?

- *Request:* Ask God to give you a true servant's heart. Ask Him to help you give, not knowing what the other hand is doing (Matt. 6:3). Ask Him to help you serve when no one is watching. Ask Him to help you give of yourself without expecting anything in return (Matt. 6:5).

- *Respond:* Jesus freely gave of Himself; live today freely giving yourself away in His name, not yours. Live in a way that expects to serve but not be served. Assault your pride by doing something for another without anyone seeing it.

DAY 15

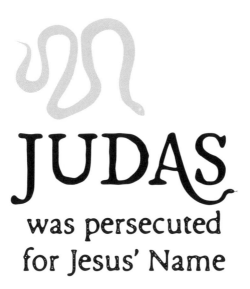

JUDAS
was persecuted
for Jesus' Name

'Blessed are those who are persecuted for righteousness' sake, for theirs is the kingdom of heaven.' (Matt. 5:10)

Each of us have favorite songs or hymns we like to sing in church. When I was in college, I attended a campus ministry called Reformed University Fellowship (RUF). Each Sunday evening after church, a certain family would host thirty or so college students for a time of fellowship, prayer and singing. The family would also feed us.

Almost every Sunday, as requests for hymns were being taken, I would ask our musicians to play *Jesus I My Cross Have Taken*. It was a song that resonated with me. There are so many rich lyrics in that song, but one particular section reads, 'Go, then, earthly fame and treasure! Come disaster, scorn and pain! In Thy service, pain is pleasure, With Thy favor, loss is gain.'These are words that are borderline insane to the world, but make complete sense to the Christian. The Christian with an eye towards eternity can welcome pain. The Christian can call pain pleasure.

Judas' persecution

Jesus is explicit that those who follow Him will encounter pain, trials, affliction, and persecution. As terrifying as this may seem, it's actually a grace from Him. It's gracious, because people should know exactly what they're signing up for when they claim the Name of Christ. This is what's a little baffling when we consider Judas.

It seems that pain would turn many off the narrow road and turn down the road most traveled, the road of comfort and ease. Why did Judas remain on a road filled with persecution if he didn't believe in the cause he was following?

Many of us could understand that Judas was interested in following Jesus when crowds were amazed by Him. When crowds were hanging on every word He was speaking. When crowds were in awe of the miracles He performed. However, when Jesus continually instructed the disciples that you will be hated by all for My name's sake (Mark 13:13, Matt. 10:22), why would he continue with them?

We know that the twelve forfeited many earthly comforts. They left their homes behind, their friends and family. They left the familiar behind; routines, contexts, scenery. They took on so much uncertainty for the name of Jesus.

They also traveled many miles to spread the fame of His name. Knocking on doors and sharing the good news of the gospel. Being welcomed by some and ignored or hated by others.

At times the persecution was light, but at other times it was more severe. The twelve knew they were a part of something significant. Even though they were often blind to the realities of what Jesus was claiming, they were probably aware that danger seemed to be right around the corner. Dissention was common. Harsh words echoed in their ears daily. It was a life many of us avoid, yet Judas embraced it.

Daily persecution

The truth is, persecution is simply a part of life. It doesn't matter if you're a Christian or not, you will face persecution. It's a normal part of an abnormal world.[1]

People are hated all the time in this fallen world for any number of things. We know bullying is a fairly common and disturbing occurrence in most schools. People are hated for their skin color. People are hated for lifestyles they choose. People are hated because they support a certain athletic team or adhere to a specific political party. Being persecuted is synonymous with being human.

Therefore, maybe the persecution Judas endured isn't as strange as we may think. Maybe Judas saw persecution of various types each and every day and thought this was just how it was supposed to be. Maybe he thought it was worth it because of the prideful fame he was after. Ultimately, we don't know.

One thing we do know, however, is that Judas lacked love.

Paul and persecution

In the apostle Paul's first letter to the church in Corinth, we learn a little bit about love. Paul, under inspiration of

---

1. This phrase is borrowed from Stephanie Hubach's *Same Lake Different Boat* (P&R Publishing, 2006), p. 27.

the Holy Spirit says, 'Love is patient and kind; love does not envy or boast' (1 Cor. 13:4). Prior to that, he tells us that a lack of love renders most things worthless. 'If I give away all I have, and **if I deliver up my body to be burned,** but have not love, I gain nothing.' (1 Cor. 13:3, emphasis mine).

It is clear that Judas lacked love for Christ – that's indisputable. However, it's also clear that he would have been persecuted for the name of Jesus. Yet Paul, writing some time after the death of Judas, tells us that you can be persecuted and it amount to nothing. You can be burned, but if you lack love it doesn't matter.

Most of us won't be delivered over to be burned for the name of Jesus. Most of us won't be beheaded for the name of Jesus. Some of us may, however. Many of us won't be imprisoned for Jesus, but some of us will. Regardless of the level of persecution we receive, we will receive persecution. The question for the follower of Christ is, *Will we face persecution from a heart of love towards Christ?*

Thinking back to *Jesus I My Cross Have Taken*, we are reminded in that song that Christians have a cross to bear (Luke 9:23). Christians are called to deny themselves and take up this cross, this burden, daily. We are called to lose our lives for the sake of Christ (Luke 9:24).

Yet, we know, *In Thy service pain is pleasure.* We understand that losing our life for Christ isn't truly losing it. We know that taking up our cross is actually a light burden. We understand that we may forfeit our comfort, pleasure, money, temporary happiness and even our very lives, but there is something much greater to come.

Judas missed this. Judas was a lover of self. All the persecution and pain Judas endured served to feed the self-rule that dominated Judas' heart. For the believer, however, we rejoice that we are considered worthy to suffer shame for His name (Acts 5:41).

Take some time

- *Reflect*: Pain is an unnatural thing for human beings. We were created for a perfect existence so pain is something we will naturally avoid. As stated, however, it must be something expected for the Christian. In what ways are you afraid of being persecuted? What's your greatest fear? Are you willing to embrace pain for the sake of Christ? Can you really say that 'pain is pleasure' in the service of Christ?

- *Request:* Ask that God would give you a heart that's willing to enter into brokenness. Ask that God would give you a heart that's unflinching in the midst of pain, persecution and suffering for the sake of His name. Ask that God would give you a heart of love that's willing to lay your concerns to the side for Christ.

- *Respond*: Live boldly for the sake of Christ today. Do not fear men and what they can do to you, fear God. Do something bold in your current context out of love for the Kingdom Christ has established for you.

DAY 16

JUDAS
gave time for Jesus

"Jesus withdrew with his disciples to the sea, and a great crowd
followed, from Galilee and Judea" (Mark 3:7)

Omnipresence is one of those attributes of God that's
impossible for our finite minds to grasp. There are aspects
of it we can understand, but we cannot fully grasp what
it feels like to be everywhere all at once. How can we
experience the awe of viewing the Half Dome Glacier in
Yosemite National Park while simultaneously beholding
the immensity of standing at the base of the Eiffel Tower
… and the moon … and all the stars … and everything else
all at once? You see, it's simply too much.

One thing we can understand as finite human beings
is the truth that we can't be everywhere at once. We are
fixed in our current context. I understand that our current

day and age grants us some sense of being in more than one place at a time. The Internet, for example, can give us the *illusion* of omnipresence. That is, we can be sitting in a coffee shop in Scotland while Skyping a friend in Brazil. It may seem like we are in two places at the same time, but we're not.

Judas wasn't omnipresent

While we currently have the illusion of being in more than one place at a time, Judas (as well as anyone in his day) definitely realized he was fixed in his current context. In other words, he knew that giving time to Jesus was taking away from other things he could be doing. When he was in the market with Jesus, he wasn't in a boat catching fish. When he was sharing a meal with Jesus and the other disciples, he wasn't sharing a meal with anyone else. He was making conscious decisions to invest his time which couldn't be invested elsewhere.

Giving time to someone or something is *always* a sacrifice. It may be a wise way to give of your time, but it calls you to say 'no' to something else. Therefore, we can say that Judas was saying 'no' to many things in order to say 'yes' to Jesus. The time he could have been giving to someone else or something else was time that he gave to Jesus.

What have you sacrificed?

If ever there was a must-read for Christians, it is Rosaria Butterfield's *The Secret Thoughts of an Unlikely Convert.*[1] For those who are unaware of her story, she was in a lesbian relationship prior to her conversion. She is now a professing Christian who came out of a gay relationship and married a pastor. As I read her story and the sincere

---

1. Butterfield, *Ibid.*

struggles for her coming to the Christian faith as well as the struggles she encountered after her Christian faith – loss of friends and community, night-terrors – my thoughts were, *What have I sacrificed for Jesus? What have I given up for my Savior? What earthly comforts have I laid aside for the Greater Kingdom?*

This story should bring conviction to any who claim the name of Jesus. What have you sacrificed for your faith? Butterfield left someone she truly loved for the sake of God's Kingdom. Judas, the betrayer, sacrificed time spent elsewhere for the sake of God's Kingdom time and time again. What about you? What are you sacrificing? How are you spending your time? If someone were to survey your calendar, what would it tell them? How often are you inconveniencing yourself to serve others? I was equally humbled by Butterfield's desire to open up their home and be hospitable. How often do you die to the ways in which you want to spend your time, to selflessly give time to others? These questions are not to heap guilt but cause grace-producing reflection.

We should be sobered by the fact that a man who currently resides in hell gave plenty of time to Jesus. I'm sure Judas sacrificed times when he could have slept in a bit more to serve Jesus. Maybe there were times where Judas stayed up late serving others in Jesus' name. Perhaps there were long days of physical labor and travel that caused him to go to bed quite late, exhausted and weary. Yet, he rose again early, before the sun came up, because Jesus had plans to move on to spread the news of the gospel.

Judas, most likely, went to bed late and awoke early at the command of Christ. What does that say to many of His followers today who can't wake up early to spend time in

His Word and prayer? If Judas did it and is no closer to the Kingdom of God, what about you and me?

Jesus' greater sacrifice

These thoughts need to convict those who claim the name of Jesus. Christians should feel conviction over the ways in which we spend our time, because it ultimately isn't our time to waste. If we are Christians, our time has been purchased by the blood of Jesus. Truth be told, even those who aren't Christians cannot lay claim to their time, since God sovereignly grants life to every living thing. Time is His.

So we need to be convicted over the ways we waste time, but we also need to see our Savior. Jesus didn't waste one second on this earth. Jesus redeemed every second by perfectly serving His Father. But His sacrifice on the cross wasn't all He did. Jesus sacrificed His omnipresence for ones who make an idol out of their current context. Let me explain.

You see, you and I are often infatuated with where we are. We love our current context. Now, I understand each of us struggle with discontentment and we long to be other places or be with other people. However, most of us are so fixated in our current location that we don't give a second-thought to those suffering on the other side of the globe. We so idolize the lives we are living that little else matters. When most of us think we're the center of the universe, why should we care about other contexts and individuals?

Our lack of being able to grasp omnipresence often makes us idolaters of what's in our presence. Jesus Christ laid omnipresence to the side to be fixed in a particular location with idolaters like you and me. The One who was present in the beginning 'began again' as He took on flesh. The One who was enthroned on high was brought low in a specific time and place. Jesus was outside of time but became One who submitted to the confines of time as He added flesh to His glory.

The truth is, we do waste time and we must repent of that. The other truth is, there are many Christians that serve God with their time but are doing it for selfish gain. They are giving time for God's Kingdom but trumpeting it to the world. In essence, they aren't relying on the perfect sacrifice of Jesus and are trying to redeem their wasted time by their own works. There is a tension here for the Christian. We definitely must strive to make sacrifices for the fame of Christ's name. At the same time, we must rest assured that the remaining time you have has been reclaimed by the righteous blood of Christ. Be confident that Christ redeemed your time and sacrifice out of thanksgiving for what he's already finished.

Take some time

- *Reflect:* Think about the ways in which you spend your time. It may even be a good idea to grab your calendar and look over your last few weeks and months. It could reveal a lot. How are you spending the time God has given you? How much of your time is spent on others? How much is spent on self? Think about it this way: if you were allowed to get off work early or have an appointment canceled or were allowed some 'free time' in some way, what would you do? This can reveal a lot about your heart.

- *Request:* Ask God to forgive you for the ways in which you abuse the time He's given you. Ask God to give you a willing heart to give time for service. Ask Him to help you give time to others: friends, family, or strangers. Ask God to help you see that all time belongs to Him and it's not ours to selfishly hoard.

- *Respond:* Go about your day today recognizing that it belongs to God. See ways in which you can give time to others. Instead of responding in frustration at interruptions, see them as ordained by God. Get involved in a ministry in your church. Take some time to be in God's Word or to pray.

DAY 17

JUDAS
fellowshiped with Jesus

'When it was evening, he reclined at table with the twelve.'
(Matt. 26:20)

I've often wondered, *Did Jesus ever get disciplined as a child? Did Mary and Joseph ever fuss at Him?* Part of me thinks that He might have. I understand that Jesus was sinless, therefore He never did anything wrong as a child. However, Mary and Joseph were sinful, so they probably disciplined Him out of their own sinful hearts. Maybe the time they lost Jesus (they lost the second person of the trinity!), they might have fussed at Him (Luke 2:41-52). Jesus' sinlessness didn't negate their propensity to sin.

In a similar fashion, we could ask why Judas didn't like Jesus. Surely Jesus was fun to be around. He was perfect in every way. Wouldn't He have perfect humor? Wouldn't He be a great conversationalist? Why wouldn't Judas enjoy fellowship with Jesus?

The gift of fellowship

Fellowship is one of the sweetest gifts of God. Sharing time with friends and family often gives us a taste of heaven. If you think about it, human beings were never designed to break fellowship and were created to share in perfect harmony with one another. Adam and Eve's sin was the first break in this fellowship. Instead of running to God after they sinned, they ran away and hid (Gen. 3:8ff).

Fellowship is something that is still sweet but is tarnished because of our sin. Friends don't know how to love and include like they should, family is often difficult to be with and we are all sinful – which results in a fellowship that is me-centered.

However, factor Jesus into the equation. Think of Jesus being physically present in the conversation or physically present at the table. Wouldn't His presence sweeten that whole deal? To be more specific, how could Judas partake of fellowship with Jesus and not enjoy it? He was literally getting a taste of heaven, but that taste was bitter to Him. In some ways I can understand.

Let's think back to an earlier quote from John Calvin: 'To know God we must know self and to know self we must know God.' This truth is telling us that the more we look at God we see His perfection, and when we look at our imperfections it helps us to grasp His perfections more deeply.

Thinking about this truth in light of Judas and Jesus in fellowship, Jesus' presence highlighted Judas' imperfections. If I can say this, it might have been a little annoying being around Jesus, because you would be constantly confronted with your sin.

When needy people came up to the fatigued disciples, every one of them just wanted to rest. Jesus wanted to serve. Whenever one of the disciples arrogantly wanted to be first and quarrels would break out, Jesus would confront everyone because of the sinfulness of their hearts.

Gift from God?

You see, it might have been annoying to be in fellowship with Jesus – not because He was annoying, but because you were more aware of your sinful heart. Therefore, the gift of fellowship with Jesus might have been more like the 'gift' of Paul's thorn in the flesh.

The apostle Paul shares about a thorn that was given to him. The thorn was given to Paul to guard him from conceit (2 Cor. 12:7-10). The thorn was a gift that was meant to foster humility. Humility is something most of us want, but we don't want the means that supplies it. That is, difficulties and trials birth humility so the path to humility is never easy.

You see, Paul begged and pleaded for God to remove this thorn, but God knew He was actually blessing Paul with this 'gift'. Paul cared more about his own comfort; God loved Paul too much to grant it to him. Instead God gave Paul discomfort to conform him into the image of His Son.

Likewise, fellowship with Jesus might have been like a thorn in the side. Think about it this way. How often do you like it when your friends rebuke you? Many times we may sincerely enjoy it and see those friends as the truest ones. However, rebukes may often beat us down and leave us asking for reprieve from that fellowship.

The reality is, by God's grace, rebukes foster humility in God's children. In the case of Judas, yes he enjoyed times of laughter in Jesus' presence. He shared in true feasting with the Creator of the very food and drink they feasted over. But his heart was at enmity with the One he fellowshiped with and that fellowship only hardened his heart all the more.

Fellowship with Jesus

Speaking of humility and rebuke, it's time for a good dose of it ourselves. We can be quick to judge Judas and scratch our heads at his lack of appreciation of fellowship with Jesus. How could he not enjoy sharing a meal with Jesus? How could he not enjoy talking with Jesus? How could he not enjoy listening to Jesus? Truth be told, many of you don't enjoy that now.

You often have a chance to break bread with Jesus now in the sacrament of the Lord's Supper, but it doesn't mean a whole lot to you. You can talk to Jesus at any waking moment, but prayer seems like a chore. You can hear from Jesus, but Bible reading and preaching seems boring. Although we cannot see Jesus face-to-face like Judas, we can partake of a unique fellowship God ordained through the sacraments and prayer and Bible reading.

However, fellowship with Jesus often confronts us with our sin. To partake of the Lord's Supper, we must be confronted by our dark hearts. To truly pray to God, we must acknowledge our unworthiness. We will be deeply challenged when we read God's Word, the Sword of Truth. Fellowship with Jesus is a fellowship of sorts with the reality of our rebellion. But, children of God see this gift of fellowship as a similar gift that was given to Paul. It brings about pain and it brings about cries for mercy, but in the end it brings about a deeper partaking of grace.

Take some time

- *Reflect:* Think of the ways in which you can enjoy fellowship with Jesus now. Church community, prayer, reading of the Word, service. Why are you hesitant to enjoy these graces? Do you even see them as fellowship with Jesus? Do you see your heart responding with humility or hardness to this truth?

- *Request:* Ask God to give you a heart of humility. See that God may be giving you gifts of thorns, that are truly gifts of grace. Ask for the same grace to be given to you that was given to Paul in the midst of his trials.

- *Respond:* Enjoy the fellowship God has given to you. Enjoy your family and friends. Enjoy the ways in which you can fellowship with God this side of heaven. Thank God for the small tastes of eternity you receive now and pray you'll long for that deeper fellowship you will experience in heaven.

DAY 18

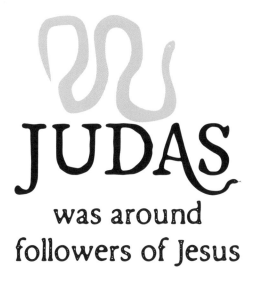

JUDAS

was around
followers of Jesus

There's a pretty catchy phrase I've seen on T-shirts and bumper stickers which reads, *God, please save me from your followers.* It's somewhat offensive, but it's something most Christians can relate to. In some ways the people we sit next to in the pews are the hardest to love. There are plenty of regular church attendees who sit in regular seats for the sole purpose of avoiding particular people.

In some ways this shouldn't be discouraging. We know the church isn't for perfect people but those who are broken. The church is a hospital, right? It's only for the sick. If that's the case, the church is going to be filled with hypocritical, judgmental, back-stabbing, gossiping, tone-deaf, arrogant liars. Maybe the bumper sticker should read, *God, please save me from your followers ... myself included.*

Not-so-sweet fellowship

In the last chapter we reflected on the gift of fellowship. Although broken, it's still a sweet gift from God. But let's not downplay the brokenness. People are hard to be around. And, truth be told, the more you're around people, the harder they can be to love.

In one particular scene of a movie I really enjoy, a young man is talking to an older man about a girl he's interested in pursuing. However, the young man states that he thinks he might back away from his pursuit. As the older man inquires why, the young man in essence says, 'Right now she's perfect, and I don't want to mess that up.' To which the older man replies, 'Maybe right now you're perfect and you don't want to mess that up.'

The older man was conveying wisdom about human nature. Yes, we may appear flawless at times, but human beings are anything but flawless on the inside. And the more you're around individuals, the more flaws you are exposed to.

Maybe Judas was put off by the followers of Jesus. Maybe Judas liked Jesus for a time, but the selfish, hypocritical liars that were following Him became too much for Judas to bear? Perhaps not, though.

A true follower

Consider some of the more positive examples of Jesus' followers. For example, what about the 'woman of the city' who entered a prominent dinner with the Pharisees? She was a woman recognized by all as a prostitute, yet Jesus allowed her to anoint His feet with her tears and the balm from an alabaster jar. As she poured tears and balm out in equal measure over the feet of the Savior of the world, the self-righteous Pharisees questioned Christ's deity. Jesus, however, praises her actions and pronounces her sins forgiven. ' … He who is forgiven little, loves little.' (Luke 7:47b)

In this scene we get a depiction of those too self-righteous to see their need for Jesus. Their own righteousness blinds them to their need for a Savior. Every Christian struggles with self-righteousness in some form or fashion and is blinded by it. However, there are those who are broken over their sin and see their need for a Savior.

The parallel account of this story in Matthew 26 tells us that what this woman did to Jesus will be told in the context of the gospel again and again. This is true in our discussion today. A woman was broken over her sin. Broken to the point of tears. Broken to fall to her knees. And, most importantly, broken to fall at the feet of Jesus.

Jesus' followers come in all shapes and sizes, because brokenness does. The church is filled with the self-righteous too prideful to come to Jesus. They feel that they're pretty well off doing their own good works. They boast before men of their heroic acts of faith.

But the church is also filled with the broken-hearted who are too prideful to come to Jesus. Frequently these church members mask their pride in false humility. They talk about how sinful they are, how broken they are, and they never rest in the forgiveness of Christ. They are more aware of their sin than the One who paid the price for their sin.

The self-righteous need to stop looking at their own works and look to Jesus', just like the broken-hearted need to stop looking at their own sinful works and look to Jesus. The self-righteous can be forgiven just like the broken-hearted who feel that their forgiveness and repentance isn't good enough. That's arrogance of another form, but arrogance nonetheless.

The woman's brokenness led her to Jesus and that's where ours must lead us. Judas was most likely the one in this story that was furious this woman wasted valuable balm on the feet of Jesus. What was in the bottle could have been sold for more money – most likely to line Judas' pockets, even though there was discussion about selling it for the poor. You see, Judas wasn't hardened by the followers of Jesus, Judas was hardened by his own rebellious heart. While the brokenness of Jesus' followers embittered Judas, he was too focused on them to see his own need.

Take some time

- *Reflect:* Read Luke 7:36-49; how are you like the Pharisees? How are you like the woman? Think of the ways in which your pride manifests itself. Think of how it manifests itself in self-righteousness and broken-heartedness. See how much you've been forgiven so that your love for Jesus would increase.

- *Request:* Ask that God would create in you a heart that's broken over your sin, yet boast in the salvation found in Jesus. Ask that God would help you feel the weight of your sin. Ask that He would help you to know the forgiveness found in Jesus.

- *Respond:* Live today boasting of the forgiveness found in Jesus. Not only let this encourage you, but treat others with the grace God has bestowed on you through His Son. Let go of grudges and love others.

DAY 19

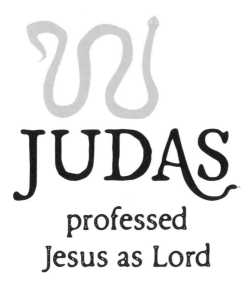

JUDAS
professed
Jesus as Lord

In Christopher Nolan's *Batman Begins*, a film that forever changed the superhero franchise, there's an oft-repeated phrase uttered by various characters – *It's not who you are underneath, it's what you do that defines you.* It's an interesting phrase to think about. It seems to follow another familiar idiom: Actions speak louder than words.

There's definitely a lot of truth in those phrases. We may even look to the words of James when he says, 'Faith without works is dead.' (James 2:14-26) Repentance and faith are synonymous to conversion, but works are vitally connected to that inward work of the Spirit.

Judas' profession
There's no record in Scripture of Judas' profession of Christ

being one like Peter's recorded profession (Luke 9:20). That being said, Judas 'professed' a lot by his actions. As stated in earlier sections, Judas endured persecution and sacrifice. He healed and taught in Jesus' name. He had sleepless nights, long days, and rigorous treks all for the sake of Jesus' ministry.

He had works to back up his 'profession' based on the lifestyle we know the disciples lived. In his case, his actions spoke loudly. Possibly, in his case, what he did defined him … at least in the eyes of the disciples. Shock, disbelief and denial were the responses of the disciples to Jesus' statement that one would betray Him (Matt. 26:22). So we know that Judas' actions professed a 'faith' that fooled the twelve.

Your profession of faith
What about your profession? Again, don't look at your verbal profession, but what do your works profess to the world?

John MacArthur shared some biographical information at the 2014 *Together for the Gospel Conference*. In his sermon he said that he had a close high school friend who professed faith in Christ, seemed to be sincere, yet later denied belief in Christ. When MacArthur got to college, he had a close friend who professed faith in Christ, seemed to be sincere, yet later denied belief in Christ. When MacArthur got to seminary it was the same scenario. He had a close friend who professed faith in Christ, yet turned away from the faith.

Therefore, as MacArthur said, his life mission has been to 'reach the reached'. It has been his longing to reach those who have already professed faith in Christ and been 'reached' by the church. His ministry has been one that's defined by this principle. To ensure professing believers are truly professing believers.

Look at your heart, Christian. Is your heart a heart like Judas? Are you one who does a bunch of work for the Kingdom, but has a heart consumed by the kingdom of darkness? Are you one who is busily involved in church ministry, but maybe deep down your motivation is for your own glory? You could be an elder or deacon. You could be a choir director or women's ministry director. You could be an ordained pastor … it doesn't matter.

Judas was in a leadership position for the Second Person of the trinity and that didn't get him into the new heavens and new earth. When was the last time, Christian, that you sat in silence and solitude, to ask these questions of your heart? Slow down and, as my pastor says, 'frisk your soul' over this thought – *Is your profession of faith merely an outward profession?*

Judas' problem

As we know, Judas' problem was that he didn't have faith. What he was underneath did define him, as well as what he did. The half-truths uttered by the earlier idioms are exactly that – half-truths. They have truth in them, but not enough. Maybe the same could be said of Judas? His entire life was a half-truth. He was filled with truth: he knew truth, he spoke truth, he acted out of truth, but he did not place his faith in the truth.

And this brings us to the crux of this book. This is the issue all Christians wrestle with from time-to-time: *Do I have a faith that saves? Am I really a believer in Jesus or am I merely going through the motions?* It is a thought we should not brush to the side too easily. There isn't a question that's more important.

Our works are important; Scripture plainly teaches this to us. If we are believers in the Lord Jesus Christ, that will result in actions done in His name for His glory. However, it is faith that saves us, but we need to be reminded that it isn't necessarily our faith, it's God's. God is the one who's faithful, not you. It is the Holy Spirit who gave you faith. It is the Holy Spirit that opened your eyes to your sin. It is the Holy Spirit that will carry you to the end. And it is this truth that fuels your works.

Judas lacked this understanding … do you?

Take some time

- *Reflect:* This chapter should cause you to take a prayerful, deep look at your heart. None of us this side of heaven are free of mixed motives. We all do things selfishly and we are sinful. However, look at your heart and see areas of pride in your service. Keep your heart suspect in your mind. Repent over your self-righteousness and ask God to give you a deeper faith in Him.

- *Request:* Ask God to strengthen your faith in His faithfulness. Ask God to give you assurance of the salvation Jesus Christ accomplished. Ask that God would give you greater repentance over your sin and that He'd give you wisdom in analyzing your own heart.

- *Respond:* Live confidently today in the finished work of Christ and let your actions profess your belief in that.

DAY 20

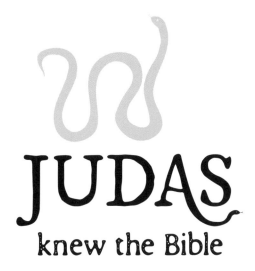

JUDAS
knew the Bible

'Seeing the crowds, he went up on the mountain, and when he
sat down, his disciples came to him. And he opened his mouth
and taught them, saying…' (Matt. 5:1-2).

I remember hearing a story of a prison inmate that was quite
inspiring. If I remember correctly, he was serving a life-sentence
and had no chance of being released. Some Christians were
ministering to him and discovered that he professed faith in
Christ. Turns out, he wasn't converted until he went to prison.
No one shared the gospel with him. No one ministered to him.
He simply opened up the Bible and began to read. God's Word
and Spirit worked to bring salvation to that man.

As amazing as this is, it shouldn't surprise us. The Bible's
testimony of itself is that it's living and active (Heb. 4:12)

and possesses a power that makes us wise for salvation (2 Tim. 3:15). Put simply, God's Word saves. It is the Bible that has the power to make the blind see. It is the Bible that makes the deaf hear. It is the Bible that turns enemies into children. Because it is the Bible that gives testimony to the life, death and resurrection of Jesus Christ. When you read the Bible, God speaks.

If the above is true, why didn't this make a difference in the life of Judas?

Judas' Bible

Let's state the obvious: Judas didn't have the same Bible Christians possess today. He was part of the New Testament era, therefore it obviously wasn't yet written. To some, this may seem like we have an unfair advantage over Judas. After all, Peter wrote that we have something 'more sure' than the prophets of old (2 Pet. 1:19).

While the Old Testament is interpreted in light of the New, Christians cannot downplay the significance of both testaments and the need for both. The New is not better. The Old and New are equal in the power and relevance and they are both the very words of God. In the above passage at the beginning of the 'Sermon on the Mount', we know Jesus quotes continually from the Old Testament and Judas was hearing the words of God from old as well as these new words forming the greatest sermon ever preached.

At another time Jesus even reads from the book of Isaiah and exclaims, in essence, this is about me (Luke 4:21). Everything in the Old Testament was pointing to a Savior, so Judas knew that Savior was Jesus and Judas was familiar with these words.

So now we get back to our initial question, why didn't this save Judas? If God's Word is so powerful, why didn't it save Judas?

In J.C. Ryle's essay on 'Bible Reading,' which is found in his work *Practical Religion*, he points to the objection by many that they have 'found no saving power' in God's Word.[1] There are those who use this as an argument against the authority of Scripture. We know this is true of our day. There are those who oppose Christianity even though they are familiar with the Scriptures. There are those who have read God's Word cover to cover and have not been changed. In fact, there are those who have read God's Word in its entirety and are even stronger in their stance against it.

God's Word today

This issue might be one that causes you to doubt sometimes. Maybe you are someone who doesn't get a sense that God's Word is all that powerful? Perhaps you aren't one who denies Scripture, you aren't one who opposes Christianity, but you are, however, a believer who doesn't like the Bible all that much.

You are someone who sits under the teaching of God's Word and completely checks out as the preacher begins to preach. 'Sermon' is a word you dread, because there's almost anything else you'd rather be doing.

Your quiet times are non-existent because you rarely remember what you read after you finished. You open up to passages of Scripture and just don't understand them. You fight fatigue as you begin a passage, because Bible reading is just cold and boring to you.

If God's Word is so powerful, why is this true of so many Christians? Why is Sunday morning such a dreaded time? Why wouldn't Christians rejoice as they enter a building to hear the Word preached and taught? Why is private Bible-

---

1. J.C. Ryle, *Practical Religion* (The Banner of Truth Trust, Reprinted 2000 [First published 1878]).

reading so difficult? Where is the power of God's Word in those moments?

A helpful reminder

The above questions were not meant to shame you in any way. I think most believers would say that Bible reading can be a struggle at various seasons of life. I think many preachers would even say that there are times when it was hard for them to be refreshed in the Word. Those who study the Bible have discussed this problem since the Bible is often an academic exercise for them and reading it for spiritual refreshment can be a challenge. All of this is to say, you're not alone.

Bible reading is often referred to as a spiritual discipline for a reason. Reading, by itself, is a discipline. It is easier to sit and stare at a screen than open up a book. There are many out there who simply enjoy reading for fun, but it takes more mental capacity to read. Therefore, reading is just going to be a bit more challenging at times.

For me, there are mornings when I can't wait to get into God's Word. It's a joy, a comfort, a blessing, and I see God's Word as a treasure. There are other mornings, however, when it's the last thing I want to do and I may not even do it.

A helpful reminder for me is this: I am dangerous. I wake up to a world that lies to me. I interact with people who lie to me. I look in the mirror and my own heart is lying to me. Lies are filling my heart, soul and mind, leaving me with no strength. God's Word, however, speaks truth. God's Word is light.

Since I am fed with lies by the world and my own heart, I need something speaking truth to me. Something that realigns my entire being. God's Word does that. God's

Word corrects my faulty thinking, rebukes my sin, imparts wisdom and fills my heart with true joy. In a sense, I'm less dangerous when I'm filled with the Word of Truth.

I think every human possesses a coldness towards God's Word. We are sinful by nature and are naturally opposed to God and His Word, so there will be coldness. Judas' coldness was fed by his own rebellion, leaving him with a calloused heart that grieved the Spirit.

However, there is another type of coldness, that wants truth. ' ... I believe; help my unbelief' (Mark 9:24). There is that coldness in your heart and mine that longs for truth. It's the conflicted heart that still speaks and thinks from the heart that's poisoned with sin even though the power of sin has been broken. It's the same heart of Paul, 'For I do not do what I want. But I do the very thing I hate' (Rom. 7:15ff).

If you are one who struggles with your love for God's Word, the struggle is a good thing. Even when you don't love God's Word, the conviction you feel over that or the desire to want to love God's Word is testimony to His Spirit's work. Brothers and sisters, we are to be people of the Word. We are to strive to read God's Word. We must pray for our hearts on those Sunday mornings and those private times in His Word. Strive by the Spirit to love and read the Bible.

Keep in mind, however, that it is the power of the Living Word that saves you, not your quiet times. Let the finished work of Jesus motivate you to read that which testifies about His life, death and resurrection. Remember, you do not read your Bible in order to be saved, you read your Bible because you are saved.

Take some time

- *Reflect:* What are some of your struggles with God's Word? Are you truly convinced of its power? Do you struggle to listen to sermons or have consistent time in God's Word? Why is that? What do your thoughts towards the Bible say about your own heart?

- *Request:* Ask God to deepen your love for the Bible. Ask God to help you see it as a treasure He left for His people. Ask God to help you understand His Word. John Owen said, our finite minds cannot expect to grasp the infinite apart from the Spirit.

- *Respond:* If you are not consistently reading the Bible, come up with a plan. Develop one today. Start with an easy book of the Bible and read it every day at a time that works for you. There are endless tools online that can help you develop a plan and help you study God's Word more deeply. Start today and start with prayer.

DAY 21

JUDAS

prayed in
Jesus' Name

'And when you pray, do not heap up empty phrases as the
Gentiles do, for they think that they will be heard for their
many words. Do not be like them, for your Father knows what
you need before you ask him. Pray then
like this ...' (Matt. 6:7-9).

Our senior pastor is very disciplined when it comes to prayer
and keeps the other pastors disciplined as he hosts a weekly
time of prayer in his office. There are some weeks we miss,
but those weeks are rare. This pastor often reminds us of the
importance of prayer, not solely by this witness, but also by
telling us all we minister for nothing if we aren't calling on
the Spirit to help.

I was twenty-four years old when I began working at this
church. Not long after that, I was asked to participate in this

time of pastoral prayer. I can remember nervously kneeling as we began this time of prayer. I was so intimidated by these seasoned pastors who spoke poetically to the Lord in their 'preacher voices.' I knew I sounded like a child and stutteringly offered up prayers to our Father.

What I realize now is, I was the only one concerned about my 'poor' prayers. Those pastors weren't judging my prayers, they actually encouraged me in what I said. And, for sure, God the Father certainly wasn't judging my prayers.

Prayer talk

Prayer is an uncomfortable subject for many Christians. I think it's confusing to many. In one sense, it's a very easy practice. It's simply talking to God. In another sense, it's a difficult, mysterious practice that often makes us feel guilty. As Kevin DeYoung says, 'If there is [something] Christians all agree on, it's that we feel guilty about not praying more.'[1]

However, we can be thankful that Jesus was gracious enough to teach His disciples to pray and that we have a record of that teaching today. From the above passage we see that many people had the practice of prayer all wrong. They were offering up 'empty phrases', thinking that their words were what mattered. Jesus, however, instructs them on what their 'prayer talk' should sound like.

As we think about this familiar passage of scripture and this familiar prayer, we must be reminded that Judas was sitting there listening to Jesus' instructions. Judas learned how to pray. Judas learned what was deemed as 'inappropriate prayer.' Judas, as one of the twelve, knew how to pray and, most likely, led others in prayer throughout his life.

---

1. Kevin DeYoung, *The Hole in Our Holiness: Filling the Gap between Gospel Passion and the Pursuit of Godliness* (Crossway, 2012), p. 129.

The practice of prayer

I find prayer to be a challenging practice. I am often humbled and convicted by my lack of prayer. Don't get me wrong, I pray throughout the day. I try and thank God for graces He brings to my attention. I try and pray about my heart and the way I judge others. I try and pray for those who are sick or hurting as the Lord brings them to mind. So I know I have a 'prayer life', but I am convicted about my ability to pray for extended periods of time.

I'm not sure about you, but I sense that social media has had somewhat of an impact on my prayer life. When I try and have times of extended prayer, I find my mind wandering. It's hard for me to stay focused on one train of thought. My mind races and before long, I forgot what it was I was praying about. Social media might not be to blame, but I sense that all the tweets and posts are cultivating minds that can't stay focused for extended periods of time.

I wonder what Judas' practice of prayer was like? Do you think he had quiet moments between himself and the Lord? Here's a haunting thought: did Judas ever think he was offering up prayers that were acceptable to God? After listening to Jesus instruct the disciples on how to pray, did he ever pray the 'Lord's Prayer' to God? Did he pray for friends and relatives? Did he thank God for the weather or a nice meal he enjoyed? Did he talk to God?

Private prayer

One can only speculate about such things. We don't really know if Judas had any sort of prayer life. If he was a disciple and if disciples were constantly being instructed by Christ and if they were called to go on mission into other towns about these teachings, it would be pretty safe to assume

Judas prayed on occasion. They were 'empty phrases' but they appeared to be prayers to those nearby.

This again is a sobering thought. Judas Iscariot prayed and still didn't have a knowledge that saved. If anything, this should move you to reflect on your private prayer. What is it like? Do you simply pray that you'll have a good day? Do you pray that you and your family will have good health? Do you often pray for safety? None of those are bad things to pray for, but they are fairly self-focused and have ease and comfort as their aim.

Our prayers reveal a lot about our hearts. Often our prayers are merely giving voice to what we worry about. Our worries are fears and fears can tell us what our idols are. Idols are things we fear losing. Comfort, happiness and safety are dominant idols among God's people. Again, these are not sinful in and of themselves, but if these are the only things you find yourself praying about, that's probably not the best practice.

Now, the last thing I want to do is discourage God's people from praying. God is a gracious Father who wants us to talk with Him about anything and everything. What I want us to be cautious of however, is offering up these 'empty phrases'. I'm pretty sure what Jesus had in mind was the 'fancy' theological words and poetic speech uttered by the religious of the day. Our caution of empty phrases is merely repeating familiar requests to God without much thought behind it.

If Judas prayed, I guarantee you he was at the center of that prayer. His concerns, desires and wants were often on his lips and they were being made known to God. The sobering reality is, that's often the same type of prayers we pray.

Christians must feel free to voice anything and everything to God; He is a Father who's full of grace we can't imagine.

However, it is His Kingdom we should be most concerned with. 'Thy Kingdom come, thy will be done' should be the truth that echoes in our hearts and minds and pours forth in our prayers. I can assure you, Judas didn't care about God's Kingdom or God's will and I can assure you his prayers reflected that. Do yours?

Take some time

- *Reflect:* Think about your prayer life and try and consider what it is you often pray for. Are you often 'worrying aloud' and simply voicing these worries in prayer? Can you discern what possible idols are present in your prayers? Do you find that your prayers are more selfish or selfless?

- *Request:* Ask God to give you a heart that's wholly devoted to His Kingdom and His will. Ask that you would have a heart that's more selflessly offering prayers for the welfare of others. Ask that God would give you greater joy and desire to be in prayer with Him.

- *Respond:* If you do not have consistent times of prayer, set a time aside in your daily routine to pray. Change up your prayer routine to guard from 'empty phrases' being offered before the Lord. Have a time of prayer that's solely one of thanksgiving to the Lord, no requests, and see what that reveals about your heart.

DAY 22

JUDAS
looked like
a Believer

' ... "Truly, truly, I say to you, one of you will betray me." The disciples looked at one another, uncertain of whom he spoke' (John 13:21-22).

Once when I was a senior in high school, I was going through the lunch-line in our cafeteria. As I was receiving delectable items from the cafeteria worker, our school's basketball coach was behind me. Somewhere along the line, he said, 'What grade are you in?' I replied that I was a senior. To which he replied, 'Boy, I could've used you.' The coach was noticing my height, which isn't ridiculously tall like many basketball players, but is a little taller than average.

The coach was obviously saying he could've used my height. What the coach didn't know, however, was that I *stunk* at basketball! Now, maybe he could have coached me and I could have gotten better, but he couldn't have 'used' me much. I looked like a basketball player to him, but looks can be deceiving.

One can make a similar comparison to Judas Iscariot. He was with Jesus Christ. He was with the other eleven. He was teaching, healing, praying, serving; anyone would have called him a disciple. On the outside, he fit the bill. But looks can be deceiving.

Works verses faith

Works and faith seem to be siblings that can't get along, at least in Christian circles. As soon as a pastor or Sunday school teacher emphasizes works too much, grace-based believers get a little uncomfortable in their seats, and rightly so. On the other end of the spectrum, those who talk about the importance of faith at the expense of works make 'doers of the Word' a little uneasy, and rightly so.

Although many like to put faith and works at odds with each other, we really shouldn't. Preachers should be able to emphasize the importance of both. Anyone who has read their Bible or grown up in the church knows we are saved by faith alone and even that faith is a gift to us from the Holy Spirit (Eph. 2:8-9). However, if the Spirit is at work in our hearts there will be evidence of that shown in our works. If there are no works to point to, that faith could be as good as dead (James 2:17).

What we have in the case of Judas is works without faith. There was plenty of works for people to point to in Judas' life. He was doing this, he was doing that. But he was doing it all from a dead heart. The question for each of us is, are we doing works from this same dead heart?

In some ways we need to say 'yes', we are doing works from a dead heart. While the power of sin has been broken in the heart of a true believer, the presence of sin remains. Just yesterday my five-year-old son asked me, 'Daddy, why do we still sin?' I told him that he was too young to be asking such questions and that he needed to go to bed. Kidding! I was astounded and thankful to God that he asked such a profound question. Is this not the question most of us wrestle with each waking hour? *Why do I sin, God? Why do I keep doing the very things I don't want to? Why can I not do the things you tell me to do?!*

In good company
One of the most comforting passages in Scripture is Romans 7, particularly verses 15 and following. Paul is dealing with the same question my five-year-old was asking, 'For I do not understand my own actions. For I do not do what I want, but I do the very thing I hate.' This passage comforts me, because the apostle Paul, the same man who wrote much of the New Testament, struggled with sin. He did the very things he hated ... time and time again.

It is this conflicted heart that's in you and in me. Therefore, we do works from this conflicted, dead heart. We teach children's Sunday school from a dead heart. We take a meal to a family in need from a dead heart. We listen to sermons and take notes from a dead heart. We sing hymns and spiritual songs from a dead heart. Our hearts are often performing all of these deeds for the wrong reasons.

You serve to be noticed. You do something good to get your name in the church bulletin. When you do something good you want someone to tell you that you did good. Your heart is just like Judas', but different as well.

What brings me greater comfort is the end of Romans 7 as it leads into chapter 8. As Paul continues to lament what a messed up individual he is, we read: 'Wretched man that

I am! Who will deliver me from this body of death? Thanks be to God through Jesus Christ our Lord! So then, I myself serve the law of God with my mind, but with my flesh I serve the law of sin. **There is therefore now no condemnation for those who are in Christ Jesus.**' (Rom. 7:2–8:1)

The difference between Judas and you?
The difference between Judas' heart and believers' hearts is war! Paul is describing a war in his mind and flesh. Judas didn't have this war. Judas was content doing works for Judas. Think about it: Jesus was a celebrity. Yes He was hated by many, but He was also loved and admired. Judas was attached to this. He received a certain amount of celebrity and his pride was stroked by appearing to be a follower of Jesus.

So war is a declarative difference between Judas' heart and that of a true believer. But there's another factor: *time.* Time tells us a lot about someone. Someone can look like a follower, someone can talk like a follower, but time will tell the truth. Time exposed Judas. It revealed a heart that wasn't at war but content with pride.

Rev. Tom Cannon has been credited with saying, 'Endurance trumps zeal anytime.' Zeal is great. We are told to have zeal, but zeal can burn out quickly. Endurance, however, reveals those who are sons and daughters of God. Those, through the years of service, the years of works for the Kingdom, the years of heartaches, who are still plugging away for the Kingdom. It is those works that are often done from a heart of faith.

Take some time

- *Reflect:* Why do you work for the Kingdom? What improper motives are feeding your works? What areas of pride do you see in your works? Do you find this war between your mind and flesh?

- *Request:* Ask God to reveal areas of pride in your works for the Kingdom. Ask God to give you endurance to serve His Kingdom. Ask God to give you strength in your fight against the flesh. Ask that God would give you a heart that serves out of faith.

- *Respond:* Take some time to read Romans 7 and 8. Think through this inner struggle Paul speaks of and ask how that manifests itself in your heart. Get involved in ministries in your church. Serve a family in your church. Do something for the Kingdom, but do it quietly and pray that you'll do it out of love for what Christ has done for you.

DAY 23

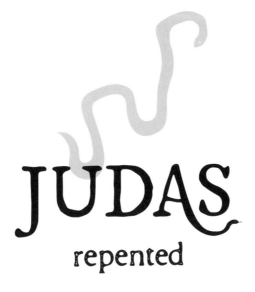

JUDAS
repented

'Then when Judas, his betrayer, saw that Jesus was condemned, he changed his mind and brought back the thirty pieces of silver to the chief priests and the elders, saying, "I have sinned by betraying innocent blood"' (Matt. 27:3-4a).

Dr. Walt Mueller, president of Center for Parent/Youth Understanding, articulated a truth about parenting I've repeated many times. He said, 'I used to be the perfect parent, and then I had children.' Many parents-to-be have idealistic thoughts about parenthood and how they would do it. They look condescendingly upon other parents and judge their efforts. I was one of those. It isn't until they have children that they receive a big slice of humble pie and realize, *This parenting thing isn't all that easy.*

One aspect of parenting that proves to be a challenge which requires a considerable amount of time is instructing a child's heart and not just their actions. 'Behavior modification' is easy; getting to the root of the problem in the child's heart requires God-given discernment and patient instruction. Simply telling your children to 'Share!' is easy. Getting them to see that they don't like to share because they're naturally selfish takes a bit more time. It not only requires the parent's instruction, it also requires prayer that the Spirit would open the child's eyes to their sinfulness and their need for Jesus. The heart must be changed, not simply the behavior.

Judas' repentance

The above passage can be a puzzling one for many. If anything, it should cause the reader to identify with Judas and have a soft heart towards him. At face value it would appear that Judas repented of his betrayal of Jesus. After all, it states that he was sorry about what happened to Jesus and he even gave the money back. These would be signs of a changed heart; i.e., true repentance.

One unfortunate reality about Judas' repentance is that we don't really have a lot of evidence to analyze. A key aspect of repentance is time (something we discussed a bit in the previous chapter), but it's something the life of Judas doesn't offer us. Shortly after Judas feels sorrow and returns the money, he commits suicide (Matt. 27:5). Therefore, we don't have much evidence to see whether or not the 'repentance' was sincere.

You see, time ultimately teaches us if repentance was indeed sincere. It's very easy for any of us to say we're sorry, but it's quite another thing for us to change our actions over time. Think of the husband who's addicted to pornography.

He can apologize to his wife, say that he's repented, but only time will tell. In the moment, there may be a form of sorrow, a form of repentance, maybe even a week or two go by, perhaps even months, yet he returns to this pattern of living after a time to prove the repentance wasn't sincere.

Please understand that I am not saying true believers in Christ don't wrestle with besetting sins in their life, sins of gossip, lying, lust, judgmentalism, laziness, but there is often fruit that accompanies repentance and often times that fruit is revealed over time. This is a complex issue to discuss and discern, but the point is we don't have much to analyze when it comes to Judas' 'repentance'.

Pro-Judas or anti-Judas?

What do you think? Was Judas sincere in his repentance? The only real evidence we have brings up another complex issue: suicide. Judas was sorrowful and chose to end his life.

As I bring this up, I understand that many reading this book have friends or family members that have taken their life. So I bring this up understanding it is one of the weightiest issues to discuss and I pray this discussion doesn't offend those reading. There are many reasons individuals decide to end their life and there are many factors that come into play when this occurs.

Suicide is always a deeply sad and tragic act, with traumatic effects for all concerned. Keeping in mind the many complexities of this issue, suicide is an act that's often self-focused. Again, I understand that there are some individuals that are going through extreme circumstances that keep them from thinking clearly. There are even those who think that ending their life is a selfless act that relieves others of the burden of their life, but this is why suicide can be labeled self-focused. Because those friends and families left behind would do anything to reassure the victim on the value of their life. The individual is not thinking about the impact this act will have on others. They're often thinking of their pain and the desire to make it stop.

It appears that this is the case for Judas. Since suicide is often a self-focused, self-centered act performed by an individual, it would give us reason to believe Judas' taking of his own life had more to do with himself and not Christ. That is, his sorrow was causing him too much pain. His suicide seems to give an indication that the pain of his actions were the primary focus instead of the pain he caused to another.

The apostle Paul gives us some understanding into this when he contrasts the difference between godly grief and worldly grief. As he's reflecting on the grief he brought God's people through a letter he sent, he rejoices because his grief moved them to repentance. He goes on to say, 'For godly grief produces a repentance that leads to salvation without regret, whereas worldly grief produces death' (2 Cor. 7:10;).

One should wonder if the actions of Judas were echoing through the mind of Paul when he wrote this. 'Worldly grief produces death' where 'godly grief produces repentance that leads to salvation without regret.' Of course, Paul has an eternal perspective on this grief, so he's referring to eternal life and death, but there is a definite connection. In reference to Judas, his grief, were it godly, would have resulted in a changed life not an action that ended his life.

Please understand that I am simply addressing the life of Judas at this point. I have known people who have committed suicide, and we are not to question everyone's salvation that chose suicide as a viable option. There are those who truly believe in Jesus and are truly saved; sadly they chose to end their life. I'm specifically talking about Judas on this point.

In light of the above section of verses from Paul, it seems to supply enough evidence for us to assume that Judas' 'repentance' was worldly because it did not result in a changed life. True repentance is seen over time and it's seen in a life that's changed. Had Judas not chosen to end his life on that day, there would be plenty of reason to assume that God had worked true repentance in his heart. His decision to end his life that day should cause us to grieve for him. The death of any human being should move us to sorrow. The knowledge of Judas' eternal life unto death beginning on that day, should sober us into reflecting on our own life of repentance now.

Take some time

- *Reflect:* This is one of the weightiest chapters discussed. Even though the entire book reflects on the life of a man who died as a betrayer, this one reflects on Judas' dying decision to end his life. God includes the life of Judas in His Word for a reason: let this example move you to reflect on your life of repentance. Do you see 'godly sorrow' in your acts of repentance? As your repentance is revealed over time, do you see a change in action? Do you see fruit of change in the sins you repent over?

- *Request:* Ask that God would give you the 'godly sorrow' Paul speaks of. When you sin, ask that God would cause your heart to break over the pain you've inflicted on Jesus, instead of the pain you feel. Ask that God would *give you a heart that is more selfless with each passing day.*

- *Respond:* It seems that many Christians today do not practice repentance. Many see repentance as the beginning of the Christian life; i.e., it's something you move on from. However, we must be repenting daily of our sins. Therefore, repent of your sins today. Think of how you've sinned against God and others and confess them to a holy God who loves to embrace repentant children.

DAY 24

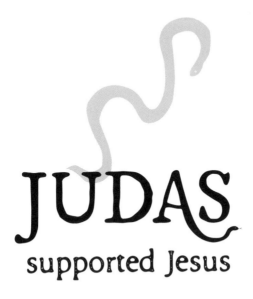

JUDAS
supported Jesus

'After this many of his disciples turned back and no longer walked with him. So Jesus said to the Twelve, "Do you want to go away as well?"' (John 6:66-67).

When I was in college I took a semester off to work with a landscaping company (I needed to experience some back-breaking labor to motivate me to stay in school). In one of my earliest days on the job we were installing a French drain system around a particular house. Shovels, wheelbarrows filled with gravel, mud and sweat were not in short supply that day. It was a long and difficult day of work.

One aspect that added to the difficulty was the fact that I was the youngest guy on the site. Therefore, I was the only guy carrying wheelbarrows filled with gravel through narrow patches of solid ground, attempting to avoid the muddy areas in the yard. As you know, a heavy wheelbarrow filled with gravel doesn't travel too well on soft ground. When my wheel discovered soft ground, as it did continuously that day, it would begin to sink and the wheelbarrow would tip over, spilling all of the gravel out. And of course I was the one who had to refill it.

Needless to say, it was a miserable day and the misery continued as the sole of my boot came off. I noticed my foot was slipping while I worked and it wasn't slipping primarily on the mud. Around the time I figured it out, my sole had completely come off my boot. To my relief, I assumed, I would get a little break to go to my apartment and get some other shoes. My co-worker (who thought he was my boss) simply duct-taped my boot and told me to keep working. Let's just say my boot was duct-tapped multiple times that day and I couldn't wait to get back into college.

Judas' support

As I discovered that day, support is an important thing. Just as my boot supported my entire body, allowing me to labor for this company, people can function in much the same way. People can add to the support of a ministry, for example. When times are tough and ministry gets discouraging, people can offer invaluable support. From the words of encouragement they speak in those tough times, to physically taking on aspects of the ministry to relieve a burden, people are major proponents of support.

I think it is safe to say that Judas was a supporter of Jesus. Based on much of what has been said, Judas gave support to Jesus. He ministered with the twelve, had specific responsibility over the money bag (John 13:29), and helped with various logistics in the ministry. Prior to the above

Scripture, I'm sure he was taking up baskets of leftover bread with the other disciples (John 6:1-15). I'm sure he was constantly helping with crowd-control (Luke 8:40-56). I would assume he had conversations with those who opposed Jesus, showing his support by refuting them. It's safe to say that he was a supporter. Again, the Scripture passage quoted at the start of the chapter shows that he continued to support Jesus, along with the other eleven, even when other disciples chose to stop following Jesus.

Although Judas was and is a betrayer (we are told that in the following verses 70-71), he was also a supporter – which sounds a bit contradictory. But let's think about this from a specific perspective. We know Judas to be a betrayer, because we know the end of the story. We know history. However, think of those moments with the twelve prior to Judas' betrayal.

Judas was supporting Jesus as one of the twelve as he walked around in amazement with the others at the extra bread that was left over from the feeding of the five thousand. As he surveyed his group of people that received fishes and loaves and collected more than he handed out, I'm sure he nudged at least one of the other disciples saying, *This is unbelievable! How much do you have left over?* Judas shared this amazement with the others. He was equally supportive and equally involved with the disciples.

His support, however, unraveled over time just like my boot did that day at work. The stress of the work day was too much for my sole. The constant weight, constant pressure and constant exertion proved to be much more than it could handle. The same was the case for Judas. I think about the parable of the sower, specifically the seed that fell among the rocky soil. As Jesus says, 'And the ones on the rock are those who, when they hear the word, receive it with joy. But

143

these have no root; they believe for a while, and **in a time of testing** fall away.' (Luke 8:13; emphasis mine).

An important side note here: we can be confident that Jesus wasn't saying true believers can lose their salvation. One important Scripture to keep in mind is John 10:25-30, where Jesus promises that no one is powerful enough to snatch anyone out of the Father's hand (verse 29). Any true believer is secure in the Father's strong hand!

Being confident that no one can fall away from the faith, there are those who appear to have a saving faith, but after a time of testing fall away. This seems to sum up the life of Judas. Just as my shoe gave way after the pressures of labor got to it, Judas gave way after the pressures of ministry.

I do not mean to minimize the awful reality of Judas' falling away by comparing it to the sole of a boot, but I think the comparison is helpful. The Christian life is often compared to a race that requires perseverance and endurance – two things missing in Judas' life.

Your support?

I've been calling you, the reader, to reflect on much of your Christian walk throughout this book. In this case, it would be *your* support of ministry. However, I want you to think about the support of ministry through the life of Jesus.

Keep in mind that Jesus was fully God and fully man at the same time. It is a reality our minds cannot fully grasp, but we know it to be true. Therefore, in Jesus' humanity, how did Judas' lack of support affect Jesus? How did the lack of support from Peter, James, and John affect Jesus? How did the lack of support from all twelve affect Him?

Speaking from experience, ministry is often *hard* and discouraging. Sometimes you can feel like you're the only one passionate about a specific ministry or you're the only one laboring for a specific area of the Kingdom. I speak from experience when I say that often these thoughts are manifested from a heart of pride. That being said, ministry can still be hard and support is needed.

Here's my point. Reflect on this specific aspect of pain that your Savior went through. When we think of Jesus' pain we quickly, and correctly, think of the cross ... but we don't need to stop there. Ministry is hard, physically, mentally and spiritually, and Jesus experienced these pains in ministry. He hurt as He saw His 'supporters' fighting over who was the greatest. He hurt as He cried out to the Father and discovered His 'supporters' were too weary to pray for their Savior in His time of need. He hurt as He saw a man, Judas, forfeit His soul after a time of testing.

We can be sure Judas gave much support to the Savior of the world. In many ways he was just as faithful on the outside as the rest of the twelve, right up until the end. However the faithful support of Peter and the 'faithful support' of Judas differ in one regard: it's focus.

If the story of Peter's life ended at his denial of Christ, we would have good reason to assume he ended up in the same place as Judas. However, his life models the reality of his heart being arrested by a faithful Savior. Judas' faith proves to be a self-focused faith that unraveled like the sole of a boot. What's the focus of your faith?

Take some time

- *Reflect:* How do you support others in ministry? Are you one who is quick to complain about minsters and ministries without getting involved and trying to serve? Are you reluctant to give financial support to those in ministry? How faithful a supporter are you?

- *Request:* Often our lack of support is birthed from a heart that doesn't trust. We don't trust that God is enough, so we hold our money a bit tighter. We don't trust that God will sustain us, so we are reluctant to give time to other ministries. Ask that God would give you a heart that's willing to give itself away in support of His Kingdom.

- *Respond:* Support your church in her worship and work to the best of your abilities. This is a vow taken in many churches, as you enter into membership. Don't be a church member that's merely a consumer. Be a church member that gives yourself away in support of the various ministries and ministers of your church.

DAY 25

JUDAS
rebuked others in Jesus' Name

'As you enter the house, greet it. And if the house is worthy, let your peace come upon it, but if it is not worthy, let your peace return to you. And if anyone will not receive you or listen to your words, shake off the dust from your feet when you leave that house or town' (Matt. 10:12-14).

As I said, when I was in college I was involved with a campus ministry called Reformed University Fellowship (RUF). It's an excellent ministry that emphasizes the preaching of the Word and involvement in the local church. God used this ministry as a vital tool for my spiritual growth and development.

Through my time with RUF, I was blessed to have two faithful ministers serve our campus. They were both faithful to disciple me, and one of the most faithful aspects of their discipleship was their willingness to rebuke me for my sin. At times I was quite shocked at some confrontations they both had with me. That being said, this aspect of their friendship was more refreshing than anything else. After all, I never had a relationship where friends cared enough about me and my spiritual growth that they would lay comfort to the side in order to have a difficult conversation with me. I loved them both for that.

Their rebukes have had a lasting impression on my soul and I've sought to model that in my own life. Without a doubt I avoid confrontation and pursue my own comfort more often than not, but I seek to rebuke and confront in the way Scripture calls us to.

As we see from the above passage, disciples of Jesus Christ were (and are) expected to rebuke and confront. As Christ gives this instruction, rebuke and confrontation are a guaranteed partner on the disciple's forthcoming journey. While we don't have an explicit instance from the above verses of Judas actually 'shaking the dust off his feet', we can assume that rebuke and confrontation occurred as he ministered.

The joy of rebuke

Some of us may scratch our heads when we see the words 'joy' and 'rebuke' together. I would doubt most people wake up each morning looking for someone to rebuke. Rebukes are uncomfortable. They're awkward. The call to rebuke is a call to lay our comforts, our desires, our wishes to the side for the sake of another's good. In short, a rebuke is a call to die to self.

I'm fairly certain that most people avoid rebuke and confrontation. Part of that is good, but part of that inclination comes from idolatry. While the former strives for the peace we were created to partake of in the Garden, the latter is fed from our idolatry of self, to have a comfortable and easy life. So, what was motivating Judas' rebukes?

Let's assume Judas knocked on the door of a house and was not received by them. A conversation had to take place, a disagreement had to take place, Judas had to voice that the truth of God's Kingdom was at odds with that particular house. Why would he do that if he didn't truly have love for God's Kingdom? I mean, it's one thing to struggle through the difficulty of rebuking someone, but to realize you're doing it in the name of Christ. It's another thing entirely to experience the awkwardness of rebuking someone when you don't even love the One in whose name you're rebuking. Why would Judas put himself through that?

This brings us to the joy of rebuking. When a person is planning to rebuke someone, there's an obvious anticipation on their part. Now this can range in levels of anxiety depending on the individual, but normal people don't enter into it lightly. Even those seasoned at godly rebukes would enter that scenario with humility. As stated, it's uncomfortable.

Therefore, there is some tension built up in the heart and mind of the 'rebuker' because they have no idea what's about to happen. *Is their friend about to get mad? Is this person going to yell? Is a relationship about to end?* Thoughts like these are swirling around. However, when the 'rebukee' receives the rebuke humbly and agrees with the rebuker, there is great relief that overcomes the individual.

Their relief, no doubt, brings about joy, but there is a greater joy for both. The rebuker and rebukee can both take joy in the growth that occurred between the two. The rebuker grew in this act because God's grace allowed them to lay their idolatry of self to the side. The rebukee grew in this act because God's grace allowed them to see the plank in their own eye. They can take joy in the grace of the Father that just occurred.

What about Judas' rebuke?

Again, there's speculation as to whether or not Judas rebuked, but I tend to think it's safer to assume he did. Not only based on the above passage, but based on the simple fact that followers of Jesus were controversial because the message of the gospel is offensive to the world. Needless to say, followers of Jesus get plenty of opportunities to confront. When you add sinners together, disagreement is the end result. So maybe speculation is a bit too strong of a word in this scenario?

If Judas shook the dust off his feet and directed a rebuke at a particular household, there was no joy. Now there might have been joy in Judas' heart from the standpoint of, *I'm glad I got that over with,* but that's it. There was no joy at growth that was taking place in his heart. There was no joy over a relationship that was strengthened. There was no joy from a recognition over the work of God's grace in that moment.

The Bible commands Christians to be joyful people. In one of the shortest verses in all of Scripture, the apostle Paul tells us to 'Rejoice always' (1 Thess. 5:16). Paul, under inspiration of the Holy Spirit, can tell the church that because the church has their eyes fixed on the finished work of the cross and the eternity Jesus purchased for them. When that reality is fixed in the believer's heart and mind, joy is inseparable from the Christian.

This was a joy that was absent from the heart of Judas. If Judas rebuked it was merely a 'form' of rebuke. A form that lacked joy. What about you, Christian? Do you rebuke others as God's Word calls us to? Even though it's uncomfortable, take heart: there is joy on the other side.

Take some time

- *Reflect:* When was the last time you rebuked a friend? This chapter isn't encouraging you to go on a 'rebuking rampage', but it is encouraging you to see the joy in rebuke. When sinners love each other they should be rebuking each other. Christians are called to love others above self and this calls us to rebuke. Why are you reluctant to do so? Is it motivated out of self-love? Fear of man?

- *Request:* Ask God to help you repent over your lack of rebuke and confrontation. Ask God to help you discern when to rebuke and when to overlook a wrong committed against you. Ask God to help you fear Him more than man.

- *Respond:* If you recognize conflict that you've avoided in your relationship, seek to confront your brother or sister in Christ. Do so prayerfully and graciously. It will be a good practice for your soul.

DAY 26

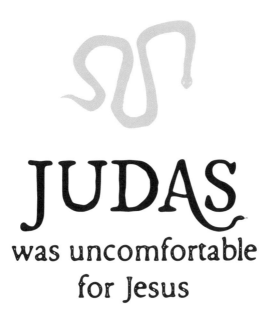

JUDAS
was uncomfortable for Jesus

'A disciple is not above his teacher, nor a servant above his master. It is enough for the disciple to be like his teacher, and the servant like his master. If they have called the master of the house Beelzebul, how much more will they malign those of his household' (Matt. 10:24-25).

Several years ago I started running for exercise. Notice that I don't call myself a 'runner'. I like to tell people that I 'dabble' in running. Honestly, for most of my life I despised running. I played soccer most of my life and running was always associated with punishment: *Perritt! Take a lap!* So, I think this is why I've been averse to the practice most of my life.

On one particular occurrence in my dabbling, I was planning on running a greater distance than I was accustomed to. I made preparations and started out on the run. In the middle of my run, I noticed some slight discomfort in one of my toes. I didn't think too much about it and continued to run. Later in the run, I noticed that the discomfort was a bit stronger, but I continued to proceed (I'm pretty tough). As I was nearing the end, I would describe the pain as a burning sensation, so I assumed I had a blister but that's sometimes expected when you run longer distances. It wasn't until I got home and took off my shoes that I noticed my white socks were red at the tip. Sure enough, my toe had been bleeding.

It was nothing serious, just some expected discomfort you become accustomed to when you *dabble* in running. However, I think if I had stopped at the first indication of pain and adjusted my socks or put some tape on my toes prior to running, I would have avoided this pain.

Pain vs. comfort

Pain and comfort are interesting topics. After all, no one seeks pain and discomfort. However, those who have read their Bibles know that God uses discomfort, pain and affliction to grow His children. We don't grow in comfortable, easy seasons of life. We grow from discomfort. But nobody in their right mind wants pain. We can understand this because we were made for perfect peace and harmony; there is a natural disdain for discomfort.

In the last chapter we saw how Judas experienced discomfort through rebuke, so let's continue to think about the discomfort he felt. Not only did he experience discomfort relationally, he experienced it by laying daily comforts aside.

Judas traveled a lot with Jesus. Traveling back then was completely different to traveling today. Judas probably slept under the stars at times. No beds, no sheets, no comforts associated with lodging at your own residence during that time. Judas probably forfeited meals as he served alongside

Jesus. I'm sure Judas got the occasional blister from travel. Achy joints from sleeping on the ground. Sunburns from the noon-day heat of the desert.

Here's my point. Many people miss out on the Kingdom of God because they are lured away by the pleasures of this world (Luke 8:14). Judas, however, forfeited so many earthly comforts and still missed out on the Kingdom of God.

Pain's purchase

I'm not nearly humbled enough by my idol of comfort. I say I love Jesus. I say I want to serve Him. I sing praises to Him. I teach for Him. *I'm in full-time ministry for Him for crying out loud!* But I serve Him from a very comfortable position. I would love to think that I'd lay a lot of earthly comforts to the side for His name, but I'm not sure – when push comes to shove – what pain and discomfort would bring from my heart.

On far too many occasions, discomfort in ministry has brought forth many unbecoming attributes of my heart. Anger. Pride. Self-pity. Despair. Depression. Bitterness. Judgmentalism. The truth is, when discomfort finds me and I don't handle it with humility, I'm declaring to God that I deserve better. *How dare you bring discomfort into my life, God! You owe me ease of life.* Now, I don't think I've ever stated it this boldly, but this is what my actions are saying. I deserve better, God.

Judas' life was no doubt riddled with discomfort. Truth be told, our modern-day minds are so removed from ancient Israel that we'd have a hard time understanding how tough they had it. However, Judas was no stranger to discomfort, but it wasn't enough to purchase his salvation. He forfeited earthly pleasures and experienced pain for Jesus' Kingdom that should truly humble each of us, but it wasn't enough.

Many of us think our discomfort earns us favor with God. *God, look what I did. Aren't you pleased with me? I gave this up for you.* There are many serving God's Kingdom today from a 'penance mindset'. The practice is subtle and the thinking goes; surely my long hours keep God happy with me. Surely my busyness proves my commitment. Look at how much money I'm giving away for God. Look at this … look at that. So much of our discomfort for God's Kingdom is actually discomfort for our own self-satisfaction. In short, we're trying to earn our salvation.

In daily preaching the gospel to ourselves we must remember that our discomfort doesn't purchase anything. Yes we are to serve, yes we are to sacrifice, yes we are to do the uncomfortable, but that doesn't earn favor with God. If anyone's life illustrates that for us, it is Judas'. The discomfort he went through for the Kingdom didn't soften his heart one bit. His hard heart never embraced the truth that the One he kissed on the cheek was the One who endured all the discomfort God requires.

Take some time

- *Reflect:* How do you react when pain and discomfort cross your path? Do you grumble at your discomfort? Do you think God owes you a better life? Do you wear your discomfort as a badge of honor? What idols does your discomfort feed as well as war against?

- *Request:* Ask that God would give you a willing heart to do the uncomfortable out of a love for Him. Seek to serve His Kingdom in a way that isn't easy. Ask God to help you embrace discomfort from Him, knowing that Christ has already endured all the pain that was required.

- *Respond:* Seek to serve your church in a way that would make you uncomfortable and require an exercise of faith; e.g., teach a Sunday school class, mentor a younger person, reach out to the unpopular or difficult to love. Christ embraced brokenness and discomfort on our behalf let's willingly do it out of thanksgiving for what He's done.

DAY 27

JUDAS
fasted for Jesus

'And when you fast, do not look gloomy like the hypocrites,
for they disfigure their faces that their fasting may be seen by
others. Truly, I say to you, they have received
their reward' (Matt. 6:16).

I like food. I even enjoy watching the Food Network from
time-to-time. If a plate of warm chocolate chip cookies and
a glass of milk are in front of me, there's a good chance
I'd finish the entire plate. A bag of Doritos in my hand
is as good as gone. I must say that I've grown a bit more
disciplined over what I eat at certain seasons of my life;
God's grace and a slower metabolism reveal that you can't
eat like a teenager your entire life.

That being said, it's hard to forgo eating. Without a doubt,
most of us in a civilized society have become so accustomed

to eating regularly that our bodies don't know how to react when we're a little delayed in consuming a meal or snack. Many of us have conditioned our bodies to need more food than we actually need.

Even though the above is true for many, food is still a necessity. In fact, that's part of the design of fasting; abstaining from something we must have. Food and drink are a must for survival. Forgo either of the two for too long and you're dead. However, fasting does teach us that there is a Bread that's more vital to life than a loaf of Iron Kids. Fasting reminds us that Jesus is the only one who can satisfy our needs.

Forgoing fasting?

Admittedly, I don't know a whole lot about fasting. I have fasted a few times in my life and it's something I've read a bit about and I want to read about more. From my limited knowledge on the subject, it would seem that it needs to be a consistent practice for Christians. We shouldn't specify a number of times per week and the heart's motives need to be questioned, but it would seem that Jesus was emphasizing a need to fast.

Christ said, 'And *when* you fast' not 'And *if* you fast.' Taking this at face value seems to lend evidence to fasting being something Christians cannot forgo. We can forgo food, but we cannot forgo forgoing food.

Fasting is intended to draw us to the Lord and illustrate our need for Him. As our bodies begin to ache and our fatigue over lack of sustenance grows, we are reminded of our ultimate need of Jesus. We are reminded that only He truly satisfies. So … what was Judas thinking when he fasted?

Even though we have a specific passage of Scripture telling us that Jesus' disciples weren't fasting like John's disciples and the disciples of the Pharisees (Mark 2:18), I would assume they fasted in the subtle manner Christ exhorts them to in the above passage. Therefore, what was Judas' fasting experience?

As Judas deliberately pushed food to the side and began to experience the pain and weakness lack of eating brings about, what was he thinking? Was he praying to God? Was he thinking about Jesus being the Bread of Life and all he truly needed? When he began to grow dizzy and have double-vision, who did he lean on for strength?

Fasting does feed us
Even though we've been talking about food, many of us are familiar with various types of fasts. Technology fasts or fasts from social media seem to be a bit more popular these days. With the advancement in technology and the portable nature much of our technology takes on, it has become such a constant in many of our lives that a technology fast is something most Christians should practice from time-to-time.

Here's the catch, though. Fasting does feed something. You see, abstaining from food or technology or anything can work against us. In some cases it can actually feed our need of the very thing we're fasting from. When you eat food regularly you don't necessarily realize how much you need it. Removing food from a daily part of your life makes you keenly aware of how much you need it.

Bill Bryson tells the story of his adventure in hiking the Appalachian trail. Much of the picture that he paints for the reader is of all the every day comforts that are forfeited for those who live life on the trail. During one of their breaks from the trail, they stop at a diner and gorge themselves on plenty of food and pie. Bryson remarks, 'Deprivation is the only way to truly appreciate anything.' To say it another way, pie is good but when you haven't eaten anything for a while and you've fasted from pie, it's even better.

Therefore, when we fast from anything it can actually increase our felt need for it. Our love for it. Our desire for it. Fasting can either feed our idols or expose them for what they are. In the case of Judas, it seems that his fasting fed his idolatry for food. He wasn't focused on the true Bread of Life, rather he was focused on his love for bread that was fed by his abstention of eating. His fasting was self-focused. His fasting only hardened his heart. His fasting fed his idolatry.

Take some time

- *Reflect:* Have you ever fasted? Why or why not? When you fast, what are your motives? What is revealed about your heart? Do you trumpet your fasting to others? Do you fast for selfish reasons? Does your fasting starve or feed your idols?

- *Request:* Ask God to give you a desire to forgo earthly pleasures for His sake. Ask God to use your fasting to help you let go of potential idols in your heart. Ask that God would reveal a deeper understanding of Christ being the only Bread we truly need.

- *Respond:* Fast. That's right, fast. It could be from food or from technology, but remove something you think you need. It will be a difficult but rewarding process.

DAY 28

JUDAS

lost friends
for Jesus

' … I will follow you, Lord, but let me first say farewell to those
at my home.' Jesus said to him, 'No one who puts his
hand to the plow and looks back is fit for the kingdom
of God' (Luke 9:61-62).

I'm pretty sure it's safe to say that we've all had friendships
that dissolved in our lives. Most likely, there were those
friends we were close to at some point, but we just began
drifting apart. There are those friendships you thought
would have lasted forever, but for some reason or another
they didn't. Maybe one of you simply moved to a different
town and you were unable to keep in touch. Maybe you
simply changed schools and changed your circle of friends.

However, maybe you've had friendships end on a sour
note. Maybe a friend started to go down a path that was

different from the one you were on. Maybe you've had friends that got into drug experimentation or a lifestyle that put you at odds. Maybe you're the one who put the relationship at odds.

There are those relationships that come and go in our lives. Having to make a conscious decision to sever a relationship is a difficult one. Being in student ministry, I've seen students follow the path of drugs to such a degree that they destroy themselves. And, the relational destruction is an added element of sorrow in this scenario. There are those friends who want to remain a friend and help, but there are those so engrossed in a dangerous lifestyle that these friends must pull back. They must choose to end the relationship, because, truth be told, there's not much of a relationship left.

A primary cost for the life of a disciple resulted in the expense of relational capital. That is, they ended relationships for the sake of the Kingdom. Some of the hardest words Jesus said were, 'If anyone comes to me and does not hate his own father and mother and wife and children and brothers and sisters, yes, and even his own life, he cannot be my disciple' (Luke 14:26). Jesus in essence is saying, 'Your love for me must be so great that your love for everyone and everything else looks like hatred.' If these disciples, Judas included, were not willing to lay aside every earthly relationship for Jesus Christ, they were not fit to be His disciples.

The familiar

I worked at a Christian boys camp one summer and it was one of the greatest summers of my life. The Lord worked on me in a mighty way and I look back on that summer with such fond memories. I would never trade it for anything, but it was also one of the hardest summers of my life.

It was physically taxing, to say the least. I worked on the ropes course crew. Part of our training was running eight miles the second day at camp. We also went rock climbing many times, did push-ups, and played with energetic kids all day for about three months. I was worn out by the end of the summer.

But one of the hardest parts of my time there was the relationships I forfeited in order to go. Don't get me wrong, I made life-long friends that summer, some of whom I still keep up with but, I also left relationships behind to go there. I remember my first weeks at camp. I arrived in a place that was unfamiliar and it was filled with a bunch of unfamiliar faces. We often sum this feeling up in the word 'homesick'.

No familiar sights, no familiar faces, no familiar (home-cooked) meals, and no familiar dialogue with friends. That was something that really resonated with me; no shared dialogue. I had inside jokes with friends, but that didn't translate to camp. Everything was foreign there.

What was it like for Judas? He said goodbye to his friends and family not knowing when, or if, he would see them again. The sights were unfamiliar, the food was unfamiliar, the group he was with was unfamiliar; he left it all for Jesus. Jesus called Judas to pay the cost of forfeited friendships and he did it. Jesus called Judas to pay the cost of forfeited familial relationships and he did it.

Judas did something most of us have never done and all of us are reluctant to do. He let go of relationships. Yet he did it for the Kingdom. He said goodbye to something of value that you can't assign a number to. He did exactly what Jesus called the disciples to do when He called them to hate all other relationships, right? Didn't Judas prove that he must love Jesus more because he pushed earthly relationships to the side? We would assume so had we not known the end of the story.

What did Judas love?

Christ's call to love Him above all else is a call to each of us. Part of that call reveals our idolatry. If we truly grasp the verse, we are exposed. Jesus shows us that we have relational loves above Him, as well as material loves that exceed our love for Him. At the end of the day, this verse should move us to repentance for our idolatry and thanksgiving that Jesus loves us faithfully even though we are proved unfaithful. But what about Judas? Didn't he put this verse into practice?

Answering a question like this needs to give us sobering pause. We can of course only speculate and we're speculating about another's heart. But one speculation could be this, however. Many people were looking for a Savior and this Savior was envisioned to be a powerful king. Jesus is the true King, no doubt. But the people envisioned something quite different. A king who was a little less meek, possibly?

Judas was aware of the Old Testament prophesies, so we can speculate that he thought he was aligning himself with a king that would move him up on the political ladder. A king that would bring him fame and popularity. A king that would bring him monetary blessing. A king that would impress all the friends and family that he left behind.

Yes, Judas paid relational capital for Jesus, but he did so expecting a return. Now, following Jesus will give us a return beyond our comprehension in eternal life! But we do not follow Jesus with our eyes focused on self. Jesus calling us to leave friends and family does not call for a 'what do I get in return' mindset. Jesus calling us to leave friends and family is calling us to get our eyes off of self. Jesus is calling attention to the only One deserving of attention. The only Savior of the world. The only One deserving of love.

Judas might have counted the cost, but assumed it would pay off for him in the long-run. He was so focused on the return that he missed out on eternity. He was thinking of all the great things he would obtain by following Jesus, but missed the fact that true greatness came from being a servant of all (Mark 10:43).

Take some time

- *Reflect:* What greater earthly loves might you have than Jesus? Friends? Parents? Siblings? Spouse? Children? What is the one thing that would hurt you to forfeit?

- *Request:* Ask that God would help you to love Him with a greater love. Ask that God would forgive you for your lack of love for Him. Ask that God would humble you by the love He lavished on us through His Son.

- *Respond:* Love Jesus by putting your relationship with Him first. Carve time out in your day to pray and read His Word. Guard the Lord's day worship of Him above earthly commitments. Do not do this to earn favor. Do this out of thanksgiving as well as being a way to obey the call of Christ.

DAY 29

JUDAS
was in danger
for Jesus

'Behold, I am sending you out as sheep in the midst of wolves,
so be wise as serpents and innocent as doves. Beware of men,
for they will deliver you over to courts and flog you in their
synagogues, and you will be dragged before governors and kings
for my sake, to bear witness before them and
the Gentiles' (Matt. 10:16-18).

A good friend of mine is a secret service man for President
Barack Obama, and he was also on detail for President
George W. Bush. As you could imagine, I pepper him with
questions. Some he can answer, some he can't ('I could tell
you but I'd have to kill you').

He's traveled all over the world and met just about anyone
you could think of, from world leaders to celebrities. Even
though that is true, he tells me that he rarely if ever actually

'meets' all these people. That is, whenever a world leader or celebrity is meeting with the President of the United States of America, he doesn't shake their hand. He doesn't say 'hello'. He doesn't even look at them. You see, the minute he looks at these people is the minute something bad happens.

In fact, most of his time with the President is spent looking away from the man in the oval office and focused on the horizon. He's not looking at the man he's supposed to protect, he's looking at the possible dangers around every corner. He's looking in the eyes of the crowd the President is addressing. Looking for something out of place. Looking for something that could bring danger.

The disciples weren't the secret service for Jesus, but there are parallels. They definitely served as crowd control and Jesus had political figure status for His time. He was a celebrity. He was mobbed by people. People wanted to be near Him. People wanted to touch Him and be healed. They wanted to ask Him questions. And, just like the President, people wanted to kill Him.

Needless to say, it would have been demanding to be a disciple. It was a job that was physically, mentally, emotionally and spiritually draining. I would assume that the disciples were pretty stressed. There was a sense in which their lives were on the line each day. Whenever they entered a town, there must have been paranoia. I'm sure the disciples spotted shady characters and wondered if violence would arise. I assume they often feared for their lives. In short, being with Jesus was being with danger.

Are you in danger?

Most of today's 'sales-pitches' for quasi-Christian religion are false. *Your best life today! Unlock the inner power of you! Riches and more are yours now!* The danger with these quasi-

Christian messages is that they are half-truths. Many of these claims are claims made in the Bible, but they take the heavenly blessings we *will* receive and claim that they can be obtained *in this life*. Not only that, but they leave out the promised pain of Christianity.

These people today are the ones Paul warned about in Philippians 1:15-17; those who ultimately preach Christ for selfish gain. These people give a false picture of Christianity, because they proclaim an easy Christianity that's absent of pain, affliction and danger. It is true that turning to Jesus and following Him will give you endless blessings, happiness and riches. But turning to Jesus will also bring you at times difficulty in relationships, animosity from your neighbor and possible physical harm.

Life in Jesus is the only true life, but as many theologians of old have said, 'The cross must come before the crown.'[1] After all, Paul wrote to the church in Philippi from prison. Stephen was stoned to death. Jesus was a man of sorrows. The disciples were in constant danger. The list goes on and on, but followers of Jesus must expect danger.

Decades ago imprisonment and violence towards Christianity seemed like a thing of the past, but the current cultural climate seems to make this more of a reality. Increased hostility towards followers of Jesus seems to be growing with each passing day. Those who hold the Word of God to be the ultimate source of truth are mocked, silenced and threatened by today's society. Much of what Christians hold to be true in the Bible is considered 'hate speech' by this world.

Let me be blunt: You are in danger. If you are a follower of Christ, danger is more of a reality today than it previously was. This comes as a surprise to some and there

---

1. J.C. Ryle, *Ibid.*

is still that branch of Christianity that seeks to deny this, but one need not think too intently to realize this reality. We call ourselves *Christians*, i.e., followers of Christ, and what happened to Christ? He was mocked, misunderstood, abandoned by His closest friends, betrayed, beaten, humiliated, tortured, and murdered. If we align with Jesus we align with danger.

This was true in Judas' day and it is true in our own. Judas did place himself in harm's way by his association with Jesus. He may have even experienced actual violence. Maybe his days of service with Jesus were filled with stress and worry over possible imprisonment and death. What we do know is that his discipleship with Jesus was no easy task. It was no walk in the park. It was filled with danger, but it was empty of commitment.

The danger Judas placed himself in each day was for naught. It didn't get him any closer to the Kingdom of heaven. This should be a wake-up call to every Christian. Many of us do not experience the danger Judas experienced, but the chances are very good that we will. Will our danger prove our profession a false one? The danger became too much for Judas. The danger made Judas desperate for a way out.

Looking to the parable of the soils again, we know there are those seeds that profess faith, but a time of testing and trials prove the profession a fake (Luke 8:13). Your security in the midst of danger is not contingent upon your strength of faith. You must recognize that danger is expected for followers of Jesus. Know that God loves His children and regardless of our circumstances brings about the best for us. By grace, fight against your idols of security, knowing that an eternity of safety awaits those who keep their eyes on Christ.

Take some time

- *Reflect:* It is normal to flee from danger, because we were designed for a place of perfect peace and harmony. However, think how safety and security have become idols in your life. What risks and possible dangers are expected of Christians today?

- *Request:* Ask that God rid you of your idols of safety. Ask that God give you a desire to take risks for Him. Ask that God help you not fear man, but fear the God who can cast you in hell after you die (Luke 12:5).

- *Respond:* Most Christians live the Christian life as safely as possible. We don't want to offend or 'ruffle feathers' and seek to be as politically correct as possible. However, the life of a Christian is a dangerous calling. While we don't need to go out and pick a fight with the world, Christians must be ready and willing to place themselves in danger for the sake of their faith.

DAY 30

JUDAS
loved money
over Jesus

'Then one of the twelve, whose name was Judas Iscariot, went to the chief priests and said, "What will you give me if I deliver him over to you?' And they paid him thirty pieces of silver'" (Matt. 26:14-15).

There was a band in the nineties that was pretty much a one-hit-wonder. Their 'hit' song contained this lyric, 'You say that money isn't everything, but I'd like to see you live without it.'[1] And this really is the tension for each of us when it comes to stewarding money. That is, we don't want to be enslaved by money, but we are dependent upon obtaining a certain amount of it each day.

Ultimately, the Christian knows their life is contingent upon God's sustaining grace, but they see money as one of

---

1. Silverchair, *Tomorrow,* 1994.

those gracious means God supplies. And when God supplies it, the Christian is then presented with a challenging level of discernment. How much is too much? How much should I save? How much should I give away? Should I give more to the church than just ten percent?

We should be humbled by Judas' example as we often see ourselves in him and this is no less the case with money. There has been some speculation in this book about the life of Judas, but one thing that needs no speculation is the fact that Judas sold Jesus for thirty pieces of silver: a slave's wage. This was all he could barter for in order to betray the Son of God and sell his soul to hell for all eternity in the process.

We already know that Judas was in charge of the moneybag and he was angry when the perfume was 'wasted' in Jesus' anointing, so we can see that he had some concern for money. Since we know he was a traitor, we can assume that he only followed Jesus for notoriety and possibly the hopes of obtaining monetary blessing.

One doesn't need to make too great an assumption to conclude that Judas' heart was driven by a love of money. I understand some may contest this because Judas gave the money back (Matt. 27:3), but we've already established that Judas wasn't repentant. He was simply sorry for how his betrayal made him feel. It was all self-focused. The love he gave to money didn't end up filling him in the end so he gave it back.

What do you love?

Idolatry is nothing knew to God's people. Judas' idol was money, among other things. But any fallen heart is going to love something other than its Creator. It's going to attempt to fill the void with something. In times of affliction, it's going to seek refuge in something other than

God. Its joy is going to be sought elsewhere, apart from God's presence.

Sadly, once the Spirit's saving work has manifested itself in our hearts, we aren't immune to idolatry. We don't love the Lover of our souls perfectly. We turn to lesser loves and commit spiritual adultery against our Savior.

Instead of loving the Creator of food, we love food. Instead of thanking God for the joy friends and family bring, we look to them as the source. Instead of looking to God for security, we think our security is contingent upon our savings account. We worry when unexpected expenses, like car repairs and hospital visits, interrupt our schedules because our security has been attached to money instead of to the God who provides it.

Judas loved money more than God and it proved to be an eternally horrific decision for him. What level is our idolatry for money on? What level are our other idols on? Here's a question: are you making war with your idols or are you content living with them? Have you become comfortable with a certain level of idolatry? Do you sense any conviction over the love you've given to created things rather than the Creator? It should be a sobering reality that the very temptation that damned Judas is present in all of our hearts. Left unchecked without prayerful searching of the heart by the power of the Holy Spirit, it can become a deadly combination.

It is likely Judas fed this idolatry for years before his heart became calloused to the Spirit's working. And along with his bitterness towards serving Christ, he serves as a sobering example to each of us. God's people must be making prayerful repentance a practice in their lives. They must be exclaiming similar cries to the Lord like those of the psalmist: 'Search me and know me, Lord!' (Ps. 139:1) We must ask for a growing distaste for our idolatry and a hatred for sin. Again, our faith isn't dependent on our ability to fight our sin, but our fighting and hatred for sin is fruit of the saving work the Spirit has worked into our hearts.

Knowing that many supposed followers of Christ lack patterns of repentance and Judas did too should be sobering. Understanding that Judas made peace with his embittered, idolatrous heart should wake us up to eternal dangers. Judas didn't lack love. Judas had zealous love for many things but lacked a love for God. Asking God to give us a greater love for Him in our hearts, above all else, is a good place for us to start.

Take some time

- *Reflect:* What are idols that the Lord has revealed in your heart? To find out what you love, look at what you spend the most time and money on. Also looking at what makes you angry can reveal your idols. Since false gods can't defend themselves, we often must defend them and our anger displays this.

- *Request:* Ask that God would search your heart and reveal the idols you love. Ask that He would help you love and treasure Him above any earthly treasure. Ask that He would give you a distaste for your idolatry.

- *Respond:* Make war with your idols. By the power of the Holy Spirit, begin to uproot those idols. Since time and money often reveal our idols, why not give more time and money to God's Kingdom this week? Serve others this week. Give money to those in need. Give away both time and money and see what the Lord reveals about your heart.

DAY 31

JUDAS
kissed Jesus

'Now the betrayer had given them a sign, saying, "The one I will kiss is the man; seize him." And he came up to Jesus at once and said, "Greetings, Rabbi!" And he kissed him. Jesus said to him, "Friend, do what you came to do"' (Matt. 26:48-50a).

Our family has watched more than a few movies where a man and a woman kiss. At this stage in our children's lives we've explained to them that a husband and wife kiss. When they get older we'll get into the details a bit more, but now whenever they see two people kiss they say, 'They're married.' Kissing equals marriage for them.

Now, I know this isn't the case at all in the day and age we live, but I'm fairly certain most would agree that kissing is an intimate thing, even to the broader culture. After all, every human being has some sort of concept of 'personal space'. That is, we don't like it when someone gets too close to us. We want space on the subway or the airplane. We get uncomfortable with 'close-talkers', as Seinfeld labeled them.

Getting too close to someone is undesirable, unless it's someone we are already intimate with. Add to this closeness, physical touch. Sharing close proximity with someone is often intimate but it is kicked up a notch when two people touch. It is one thing for two people to brush shoulders, but an entirely different category when they hold hands. If this is true, then two people sharing close proximity and touching lips together is, indisputably, intimate.

The kiss of death

No matter what our culture says and what social mores they've come to accept, kissing is intimate. You're in someone's space, you're touching them, and you're not merely touching, you're touching lips. Now, I understand that Judas didn't touch lips with Jesus, but he shared something intimate with the Son of God in order to betray Him.

One of the most intimate of human experiences was used as a signal to turn the Son of God over to His destroyers. This kiss would notify the guards who to mock, ridicule, beat, scourge and nail to a cross. This kiss would bring separation between Jesus and His disciples. This kiss would be the moment Jesus' entire life has been building up to. This kiss of death, however, would bring God's plan of redemption to fruition.

This kiss signified death. It signified death for Jesus. It was part of the plan Judas had discussed with the guards. It signified death for Judas. He looked one last time into the eyes of the Man who could save him and simply turned him over. It signified the death of death. Three days later, Christ would roll away the stone and walk away from that tomb. It signified the death of life as we know it. This earth is now closer to its end but the beginning of life eternal is ready for its beginning.

The 'kiss' of Christ

The beautiful hymn, *When I Survey the Wondrous Cross*, contains these rich lyrics that reflect upon the Savior on the cross, 'Did e'er such love and sorrow meet? Or thorns compose so rich a crown?'. Two polar opposites coming together: love and sorrow; sharp thorns and rich crown … kiss and betrayal. These things didn't belong together, but they were brought together through the man Jesus Christ.

Judas disgraced the kiss by using it to betray the Savior of the world. The kiss did not deserve to be disgraced in the manner Judas did. Judas betrayed with a kiss. The greatest traitor in human history kissing the most faithful and trustworthy. Christ, however, has a kiss of His own. What is the 'kiss' of Christ? The kiss of Christ is epitomized in the reality of the divine God 'kissing' humanity by becoming a human being. Jesus the King became Jesus the babe. The Creator became creature by taking on flesh, leaving His throne and coming to dwell with sinful man. The King of Glory does not belong among prostitutes, tax collectors and self-righteous Pharisees, yet He humbled Himself and dwelt among them.

King of contrasts

What else doesn't belong together? Enemies adopted as children. You see, God has a way of reconciling things that don't belong. Judas abused the kiss but God used it to bring His plan of redemption to completion. Christ's disciples argued about who was the greatest, but Christ became the least so we could inherit the Kingdom. Leaders don't serve and servants don't lead, but Jesus led by serving, reconciling what doesn't belong together. Giving away something is losing, but Christ reconciled giving as receiving.

Any one of us can see a lot of ourselves in Judas. He was an idolater and so are we. He feared man and so do we. He lacked faith and so do we. He sinned against Jesus and so do we. We should be humbled as we survey the life of Judas and realize our lives are often anything but faithful. However, we serve a Savior of reconciliation and He's the faithful one that reconciles the faithless to Himself.

Take some time

- *Reflect:* What are your doubts about the salvation Jesus purchased? Where do you lack assurance? Do you doubt that Jesus could save a sinner like you? Are you on the other end of the spectrum; do you rarely give a second-thought to your sin and what your Savior has accomplished? We don't need to be too consumed with our sin that we fear salvation, but we don't need to be too proud that our sin doesn't humble us.

- *Request:* Ask that God would humble you in your sin. Ask that He would give you confidence in His reconciling work on the cross. Ask that He would remove any doubt of salvation. Ask that He would work a humble boasting into your heart; the two things that are reconciled by the cross.

- *Respond:* Preach the gospel to yourself today. Live today knowing that there is no condemnation for those in Jesus (Rom. 8:1). Tell yourself that Jesus became poor so that you could be rich (2 Cor. 8:9). Believe that

Jesus took the punishment for sin on the cross so that you would obtain righteousness (2 Cor. 5:21). Live in the freedom of the gospel right now and ask that God would make it resonate in your heart and mind every day.

CONCLUSION

It has been an interesting task to reflect on the life of a man who betrayed the only perfect man. To assume what the eyes, ears and hands of Judas must have witnessed while walking in step with the Son of God is a weighty thing. To think about the heart of a man who was heartless towards the Messiah is difficult … but then again, it's not too much of a stretch from my own heart.

Much of my desire to write this was because of my own heart. As I've inferred throughout, I have doubts at times over my salvation. I would assume that you do as well. Sometimes I wonder if I'm really saved. Sometimes I wonder if the faith I claim was the same 'faith' Judas appeared to have. On the day of my death or the day the Lord returns, am I going to hear, 'Well done, good and faithful servant' (Matt. 25:21)? Or, 'I never knew you depart from me.' (Matt. 7:23)?

The Christian can rest assured in the saving grace of Jesus Christ and the confidence that He is faithful to sustain and keep us in His grip (John 10:28-30). That being said, our hearts are poisoned with sin and we therefore are filled with doubts. While Christians need to have assurance of salvation, they need to question their salvation at times. I am not saying to question the power or the source. I'm simply saying they need to look at their heart.

Judas has been in eternal torment since he hung himself. He has never had a moment of peace, happiness, joy or rest since his soul descended into hell nor will he ever experience those moments for the eternity to come. His life has been filled with unending sorrow, suffering, pain, loss and fear and his life will continue down that same course for time eternal. Because eternity is a reality that possesses only two outcomes, pausing to think about the condition of one's heart is a worthwhile exercise. I hope this little devotional assisted you to that end.

Eternity is beyond our finite minds, yet it is worth stretching ourselves to consider. Brothers and sisters, what could be more important? I hope the similarities between your life and Judas' have at least given you pause. I hope you've seen yourself in him. I pray you've repented in certain areas and renewed your faith in others. I pray that the Holy Spirit has brought about humility over your sin.

I firmly believe that the life of Judas was sovereignly recorded in Scripture to give us pause. To move us to analyze our faith and search our hearts. Don't let this example from Scripture leave you unmoved. I pray that God uses the example of Judas to move you to a more certain faith in Christ. I pray that God uses the example of Judas to spur you on to sharing the gospel with your unbelieving friends and neighbors knowing of the eternity that awaits. I pray that God uses the example of Judas to wake us up to what's really important in life.

* * *

When Christian Focus graciously agreed to publish this book, I had only submitted five or so sample chapters to them. I honestly didn't know what the rest of the book would contain or what the ensuing months would hold as I began deeper reflection into Judas' life. I knew there was some sobriety and pity in my heart for this man I'll never meet. It's strange, but I think I can now say that I hold a certain level of gratitude for Judas, if that can be said. I feel strange saying that, because he was a betrayer, a hater of Jesus, a lover of self and a man that attempted to destroy Christianity as we know it. Simply subtract God's grace from my life however, and I'm Judas.

I'm grateful that God works good out of evil and that's why I'm grateful for the life of Judas. More importantly, I'm grateful for the God who worked 'Judas' out of my own heart and gave me a heart that loves Him. I trust you are, too.

While we've been reflecting on the question, *What would Judas do?*, we know with certainty what Jesus Christ did do. Jesus left His throne, took on flesh, lived the life we could not live and died the death that we deserve. This is what Jesus did for true believers who look and act a little like Judas at times.

JOHN
PERRITT

YOUR **DAYS**
ARE NUMB3RED

A CLOSER LOOK AT HOW
WE SPEND OUR TIME
& THE ETERNITY BEFORE US

YOUR DAYS ARE NUMBERED
A closer look at how we spend our time
and the eternity before us
by John Perritt

Wasting time might not seem like a big deal to some, except for the fact that our time really isn't ours, but God's. Not only that, but it is a limited resource. You can be the richest person in the world and you still can't buy more time.

If we want a heart of wisdom, according to the psalmist, we must number our days. *Your Days are Numbered* takes a biblical look at the way in which we spend our time to cultivate this mind-set of seeing each day as a vital opportunity to live for the glory of God.

> In a culture that spends its days killing time, wasting time, or managing time, John Perritt urges us to become intentional about how we number our days. He does so not from a sense of guilt or manipulation, but from a rich Gospel basis.
>
> *Sean Michael Lucas, Senior Pastor,*
> *Independent Presbyterian Church, Memphis, Tennessee*

> ... so much wise and godly counsel in this book. He challenged me to consider my priorities so I can love God and love my neighbors with all my heart, soul, mind, and strength. No doubt he'll do the same for you.
>
> *Collin Hansen, Editorial Director,*
> *The Gospel Coalition and author of "Blind Spots"*

> ... This is essential reading for those concerned with addressing the question, 'How may I glorify God in the legitimate pursuit of leisure?' I heartily recommend it.
>
> *Derek Thomas, Senior Minister of Preaching and Teaching,*
> *First Presbyterian Church, Columbia, South Carolina*

ISBN: 978-1-78191-744-2

HEAVEN, HOW I GOT HERE

THE STORY OF THE THIEF ON THE CROSS

COLIN S. SMITH

Heaven, How I Got Here
The Story of the Thief on the Cross
by Colin S. Smith

What if you woke up one morning knowing that it was your last day on earth? That's what happened to the thief on the cross, who died a few feet from Jesus. *Heaven, How I Got Here* is his story, told in his own words, as he looks back from Heaven on the day that changed his eternity, and the faith that can change yours.

> ... brilliant idea beautifully executed ... combines pastoral wisdom and narrative skill to help us get inside the heart and mind of the thief on the cross, crucified next to the Christ on Calvary.
> *Justin Taylor, Executive vice president,*
> *Crossway Books and blogger, "Between Two Worlds",*
> *Wheaton, Illinois*

> I've never read anything like this! This compelling first-person account from a heavenly perspective helped me understand and appreciate what Jesus endured on the cross and why he did it.
> *Collin Hansen, Editorial Director,*
> *The Gospel Coalition and author of "Blind Spots"*

> Here is a gripping account of God's amazing grace that comes alive as recounted from this unusual and really helpful perspective.
> *Alistair Begg, Senior Pastor,*
> *Parkside Church, Chagrin Falls, Ohio*

> How I wish that every skeptic and every believer would read this book!
> *Erwin Lutzer, Senior Pastor,*
> *Moody Church, Chicago, Illinois*

ISBN: 978-1-78191-558-5

Christian Focus Publications

Our mission statement –

STAYING FAITHFUL
In dependence upon God we seek to impact the world through literature faithful to His infallible Word, the Bible. Our aim is to ensure that the Lord Jesus Christ is presented as the only hope to obtain forgiveness of sin, live a useful life and look forward to heaven with Him.

Our books are published in four imprints:

CHRISTIAN
FOCUS

Popular works including biographies, commentaries, basic doctrine and Christian living.

CHRISTIAN
HERITAGE

Books representing some of the best material from the rich heritage of the church.

MENTOR

Books written at a level suitable for Bible College and seminary students, pastors, and other serious readers. The imprint includes commentaries, doctrinal studies, examination of current issues and church history.

CF4·K

Children's books for quality Bible teaching and for all age groups: Sunday school curriculum, puzzle and activity books; personal and family devotional titles, biographies and inspirational stories – Because you are never too young to know Jesus!

Christian Focus Publications Ltd,
Geanies House, Fearn, Ross-shire,
IV20 1TW, Scotland, United Kingdom.
www.christianfocus.com